BASIC ENDGAME STRATEGY

ROOKS & QUEENS

ABOUT THE AUTHOR

Bill Robertie is a chess master and a former winner of the US Chess Speed Championships. He is also the world's best backgammon player and the only two-time winner of the Monte Carlo World Championships. Besides authoring six books on chess, the first in a series of more than 10 titles in *The Road to Chess Mastery Series*, he's written six books on backgammon and is the co-publisher of *Inside Backgammon*, the world's foremost backgammon magazine.

His club and tournament winnings from chess and backgammon allow Robertie to travel the world in style. Robertie currently makes his home in Arlington, Massachusetts.

BACKGAMMON AND CHESS BOOKS BY BILL ROBERTIE

Chess Books
Beginning Chess Play
Winning Chess Tactics
Winning Chess Openings
Master Checkmate Strategy
Basic Endgame Strategy: Kings, Pawns, & Minor Pieces
Basic Endgame Strategy: Rooks & Queens

Backgammon Books
Backgammon for Winnersc
Backgammon for Serious Players
Advanced Backgammon Volume 1: Positional Play
Advanced Backgammon Volume 2: Technical Play
Lee Genud vs. Joe Dwek
Reno 1986

BASIC ENDGAME STRATEGY

STRATEGY

ROOKS & QUEENS

BILL ROBERTIE

- ROAD TO CHESS MASTERY -
CARDOZA PUBLISHING

CARDOZA PUBLISHING
Authoritative and Readable Books for Chess Players
- Chess is Our Game -

Cardoza Publishing is the foremost gaming and gambling publisher in the world with a library of almost 100 up-to-date and easy-to-read books and strategies. These authoritative works are written by the top experts in their fields and with more than five million books in print, represent the best-selling and most popular gaming books anywhere.

First Edition

Library of Congress Catalog Card No: 97-94720
ISBN:0-940685-89-2

CARDOZA PUBLISHING
P.O. Box 1500, Cooper Station, New York, NY 10276
(718)743-5229 • email: cardozapub@aol.com

Write for your <u>free</u> catalogue of gaming books,
advanced strategies and computer games.

Visit our web site: www.cardozapub.com

TABLE OF CONTENTS

1. INTRODUCTION

While it's a lot of fun to win a chess game in the early stages, with a quick, decisive checkmating attack or a combination that wins a lot of material, it doesn't always happen that way. Sometimes your opponent will match you move for move and idea for idea.

When that happens, you can't get discouraged. A true competitor is willing to battle to the last pawn to try to squeeze out a win. And sometimes, that's exactly what you have to do.

When your opponent does put up a tough fight, the battle may last into the endgame. When it does, you'll need to know the key strategies that lead to endgame victories. That's the job of this book.

I'll show you what you need to know to squeeze out a win when both sides have been reduced to just a Rook and a few pawns, or a Queen and a few pawns. These positions might look simple at first, but they're full of traps for the unwary. With the lessons in this book, you'll be the player setting the traps, and your opponents will be turning over their Kings in surrender.

Let's get started!

2. CHESS NOTATION

Chess notation is a simplified way of recording the moves in a chess game. By learning chess notation, you'll be able to follow the games and explanations in this or any other chess book. It's really quite easy. Here's how it works.

Chess notation starts by putting a coordinate grid over the chessboard. Take a look at the diagram below.

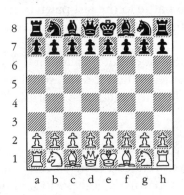

Diagram 1: The Notation System

THE NOTATION SYSTEM

The horizontal rows, or ranks, are numbered from 1 to 8. White's first row, the rank containing the White pieces, is number 1. The rank with Black's pieces is now number 8. The vertical rows, or files, are lettered "a" through "h", with "a" starting on White's left and "h" on White's right.

This grid system lets us refer to any square on the board by a unique name. White's King is currently sitting on the square "e1". Black's Queen is on square "d8", and so on. In addition to the grid system, we have abbreviations for each of the pieces. Here they are:

ABBREVIATIONS FOR THE PIECES

King	K
Queen	Q
Rook	R
Bishop	B
Knight	N
Pawn	-

To indicate a move, we write down the piece that moved, and the starting and ending squares of the move. However, if a pawn is moving, we don't need to write anything more than the starting and ending squares. We use a dash to separate the starting and ending squares, and an "x" if the move was a capture.

SPECIAL NOTATIONS

Certain moves in chess have their own special notation:

• Castling King-side is denoted by "0-0". Castling Queen-side is denoted by "0-0-0".

• When promoting a pawn, indicate the promoted piece in parentheses: for instance, "a7-a8(Q)" says that white moved a pawn to the a8 square and promoted it to a Queen.

• Capturing en passant is denoted by "ep" after the move; for instance, "d5xc6 ep" shows a pawn capturing en passant on the c6 square.

We use exclamation points and question marks to comment on the ingenuity or effectiveness of moves. Here's what they mean:

ANNOTATION COMMENTS

! means a good move.
!! means a brilliant, completely unexpected move.
? means an error.
?? means a gross blunder, probably losing the game.

---

3. ENDGAMES WITH MAJOR PIECES

In the companion volume to this book, "Basic Endgame Strategy: Kings, Pawns, and Minor Pieces," we explained the differences between middlegame play and endgame play. Although that book talked about endings with Bishops and Knights on the board, the difference might apply just as well to endings with Rooks and Queens (the "major pieces"). Here's a recap of the major differences:

DIFFERENCES BETWEEN ENDGAMES & MIDDLE GAMES

(1) The King is a fighting piece. In the opening and middle game, the King is a weak piece, the target of the enemy's attacks. But when the number of pieces have been reduced to one or two, the King isn't in much danger. Now the King is a powerful asset, able to wreak havoc when set loose among enemy pawns. The first step in a well-played ending is usually to centralize the King, to use him as a fighting piece on either side of the board.

(2) Pawns are critical. In the middlegame, pawns can be used to control space, or as battering rams to punch open enemy defenses. But for the most part, pawns play a supporting role.

In the endgame, pawns become the key to victory. Pushing a pawn to the eighth rank and promoting it to a Queen will force your opponent's capitulation.

(3) Queening combinations. In the book "Winning Chess Tactics," I explained how to win a chess game using a whole basketful of tactical ideas, including Knight forks, double attacks, discovered checks, and overworked pieces.

In the endgame, with not many pieces on the board, a lot of these tactical ideas aren't available. A new tactical idea (that doesn't usually occur in the middlegame) becomes critically important: Forcing a pawn through to Queen.

(4) Stalemate. Getting a draw with a stalemate isn't possible in the opening or the middlegame — the losing side has too many pieces to move. But in the ending, where the losing side might have just a King and one other piece plus some blocked pawns, arranging a stalemate to save the game is a common theme.

STRATEGY WITH ROOKS AND QUEENS

On the one hand, endgames with Rooks and Queens aren't all that different from other endgames. The King is still a fighting piece and needs to be mobilized, even though he'll be in a bit more danger with Rooks or Queen roaming around the board than he was facing weaker Knights or Bishops. Forcing a pawn through to Queen is still the main idea, and Queening combinations are often the key winning maneuver. Also, the defending side will still try to save himself with a creative stalemate trap when the opportunity arises.

However, there are a couple of strategic ideas that are unique to these major piece endings. Try to learn them, and notice how they're used in the endings that appear later in this book.

(5) Activate the Rook. In Rook endings, an active Rook is usually the key to victory, often even more important than an extra pawn. You want your Rook attacking key enemy pawns, forcing your opponent to use his valuable Rook to defend his pawns. You also want your Rook restricting the enemy King, confining him to the rear ranks or files along the edge of the board.

In endings with Bishops or Knights, the first strategic moves were usually spent centralizing the King. In Rook endings, the top priority is maneuvering to activate your Rook and to force your opponent into passivity. Only then do you bring the King into play. By following the examples in this book, you'll learn how to time and execute these maneuvers yourself.

(6) Create a passed pawn. With major pieces on the board, passed pawns are especially powerful. A Queen plus a passed pawn is an irresistible threat. Even an opposing Queen can't stop their advance. A passed pawn supported by a Rook behind it is almost as strong; your opponent can block the pawn with his Rook, but at the cost of tying his Rook down for the rest of the game.

In Rook and Queen endings, the play revolves around getting a passed pawn, pushing it as far as possible, then figuring out how to break through the defender's blockade. In this book, you'll learn all the secrets of these maneuvers.

THE LAYOUT OF THIS BOOK
We'll start in Chapter 4 by showing you how to stop an advanced pawn or two with your Rook.

Chapter 5 covers the important endgame of Rook and pawn against Rook. We'll show you the basic positions that are draws, then the key maneuver that lets the stronger side force a win from a good position.

In Chapter 6, we'll look at complex positions where Rook battles Rook with many pawns on the board. The key idea in these endings is an active Rook position. We'll show you how to achieve an active position and make good use of it.

If a single pawn is far enough advanced, even a Queen can have trouble stopping it. Chapter 7 shows when the Queen can win and when the pawn can draw.

Chapter 8 covers endings with Queen and pawn against Queen. In some cases, the Queen and pawn can force a win. We'll show you how.

Endings with Queens and many pawns are covered in Chapter 9. An advanced passed pawn is a tremendous advantage in these endings, even more important than an extra pawn.

Chapter 10 looks at endings where a Queen battles against two Rooks. Usually these endings favor the Rooks, especially if the board is wide-open. You'll learn how to take advantage of these special situations.

Let's get started!

4. ROOK AGAINST PAWNS

Suppose you are winning an ending where you have a Rook and a single pawn (and a King of course) and your opponent has the same material. Your pawn is farther advanced, so you push it up the board and make a Queen. Your opponent naturally gives up his Rook for your Queen, and you recapture. Now you have a Rook left, and he just has a pawn.

Can you win this ending? Will your Rook and King be able to cooperate, stop his pawn, and finally capture it, or will your opponent be able to draw the game?

Mostly, you should be able to win this endgame, but your Rook and King will have to work together efficiently. Let's see how it's done.

ROOK AGAINST ONE PAWN

The battle of a Rook against a single pawn can be a close affair. Suppose that White has the Rook and Black has just a single pawn. In order to win the game, White's King and Rook will have to cooperate. If the White King is close enough so that the King and Rook can both control some square that the pawn has to cross, then White can eventually capture the pawn and checkmate with the Rook. If White's King is too far away, or if the Black King can somehow fend off the White King, Black can draw the game by Queening his pawn and forcing White to exchange his Rook for the new Queen.

Take a look at Position 2.

Diagram 2: Black on Move

The White King and the Black pawn are both racing for the Queening square, b1. Can White make it in time? Just barely, but he has to know a couple of tactical tricks to win the game. Let's watch how White handles matters.

>	1	...	b5-b4

There's no subtlety in Black's play. He just pushes the pawn as fast as he can.

>	2	Kg4-f3

White heads for b1 by the most direct route.

>	2	...	b4-b3

Will Black get there first?

>	3	Kf3-e2

If Black now plays 3 ... b3-b2, White moves 4 Ke2-d1, and Black's King has to leave the protection of the pawn. So Black needs to keep the White King at a distance.

3   ...   Kc3-c2!

Keeps out the White King and threatens to Queen the pawn.

4   Rb8-c8 check!

This is the key maneuver in this ending. White makes progress by checking with his Rook, forcing the Black King to give ground.

4   ...   Kc2-b2
5   Ke2-d2

Getting closer.

5   ...   Kb2-a2

Now the pawn is free to advance again.

6   Kd2-c3

Once the White King gets next to the pawn, White's almost home.

6   ...   b3-b2
7   Rc8-a8 check   Ka2-b1

Black is forced to block his pawn, but he has one last trap in mind.

8   Ra8-b8

This ensures the capture of the pawn.

8   ...   Kb1-a1!

Diagram 3: White on Move

Do you see the trap? If White blindly plays 9 Rb8xb2??, Black is stalemated in the corner!

Can White still win? Yes, but he needs one last finesse.

      9   Kc3-c2!

This is it. Now White gets to capture the pawn with check, thus avoiding stalemate.

      9   ...   b2-b1 (Q) check
     10   Rb8xb1 check

And White will force checkmate in a few moves.

The win isn't always that tricky. Sometimes White can use his Rook to prevent the Black King from helping his pawn. When that happens, the pawn can get in trouble on its own. Take a look at the next position.

Diagram 4: White on Move

White's King is far away, which is a problem for him. But Black's King and pawn are far away from the Queening square, which is a really big problem for him. In fact, it allows White to win the game quite easily, if he sees the right idea.

> 1   Rb7-b5!

Here it is. White controls the entire fifth rank with his Rook, so the Black King can't make any progress towards the Queening square. That means the pawn will have to make its way on its own, a tough task for a pawn matched up against a powerful Rook.

> 1   ...   h6-h5

There's no way Black can improve the position of his King, so there's nothing to do but let the pawn march.

> 2   Kb8-c7   h5-h4
> 3   Kc7-c6   h4-h3

Once the pawn gets too far from the King, the Rook steps in for the kill.

4   Rb5-b3!

Attacking the pawn, which can't be defended.

4   ...   h3-h2

Almost!

5   Rb3-h3

That's it. The Rook captures the pawn next turn.

ROOK AGAINST TWO PAWNS

When one side has two pawns against a Rook, the game becomes considerably more interesting. If the pawns are far enough advanced, they may even defeat a Rook! Take a look at the next position:

Diagram 5: Black on Move

Black's King is far away from the action, while the pawns are fairly far advanced. The Rook can put up a fight, but eventually the pawns will triumph.

1   ...   Ra1-f1

The right idea for Black is to attack the leading pawn. This freezes both pawns in their tracks. If either one moves, Black captures the f-pawn first, then picks up the g-pawn later.

2	Ke3-d4!

With the pawns immobilized, White brings up the King to assist. By moving to d4, rather than e4, he keeps the Black King blocked out of c3.

2	...	Kb2-b3

Black tries to get the King closer.

Black has another idea which almost works. He could have played 2 ... Rf1-f5, attacking the g-pawn. If the g-pawn advances, Black could take the f-pawn. But White could still win by playing 3 Kd4-e4! Rf5xg5 4 f6-f7, and Black can't reach the Queening square.

3	Kd4-e5

Once the White King can support the two pawns, Black is in trouble.

3	...	Kb3-c4
4	g5-g6	

As a rule, if White can get both his pawns to the sixth rank, he can win. That's the case here.

4	...	Rf1-e1 check
5	Ke5-d6	Re1-g1
6	g6-g7	

The pawns advance steadily.

6	...	Kc4-d4

Black is trying to get to the Queening squares, but the White King blocks the most direct route.

Diagram 6: White to Move

7   Kd6-c6!!

This apparently nonsensical move is actually the only way to win. What's wrong with the obvious 7 Kd6-e6? Black would reply 7 ... Kd4-e4, and then White has a couple of choices:

One idea would be to escort the pawns in with the King, by playing 8 Ke6-f7. But Black would play 8 ... Ke4-e5, attacking the rear pawn with his King, and after 9 g7-g8 (Q) Rg1xg8 10 Kf7xg8 Ke5xf6, Black has managed to exchange off all the pawns and get a draw.

The other idea would be 8 f6-f7, hoping that Black would capture, 8 ... Rg1xg7, after which White Queens on f8 with an easy win. But Black wouldn't capture on g7! Instead, he would play 8 ... Rg1-g6 check! White would have to move forward, 9 Ke6-e7, and Black would play 9 ... Rg6xg7, capturing one pawn while pinning another. Next turn he'd capture on f7, again with a draw.

This last variation shows the key to the winning idea, however. White doesn't need his King in the immediate vicinity of the pawns to force a Queen — the pawns can do that all by themselves. White has to make sure that when Black checks on g6, White doesn't have to play his King up to the seventh rank. He needs to be able to play back to the fifth rank, so that his pawn on f7 can't get pinned. That means he has to get his King away from Black's King. Hence, the weird-looking move 7 Kd6-c6, aiming to get the King over to b5.

| 7 | ... | Kd4-c4! |

If White wants to get out to b5, Black has to stop him. The Black King can't help stop the pawns anyway.

| 8 | Kc6-d7! | |

A new idea — the King heads directly for the square e8, where it can force through the f-pawn. Black is one move too late to stop this plan.

8	...	Kc4-d5
9	Kd7-e8	Kd5-e6
10	f6-f7	

One of the White pawns will Queen, but Black still has a resource left.

| 10 | ... | Rg1-a1 |

Diagram 7: White on Move

Oops. Has White checkmated himself? If either pawn Queens, Black plays Ra1-a8 checkmate. If White tries Ke8-d8, Black plays Ke6xf7 and gobbles up the other pawn with an easy win. What can White do?

11	f7-f8 (N) check!!

This is White's trick. By underpromoting the f-pawn to a Knight, he chases the Black King away from e6 with a check.

11	...	Ke6-f6
12	g7-g8 (Q)	Ra1-a8 check
13	Ke8-d7	

And White will win.

5. ROOK & PAWN AGAINST ROOK

In this chapter, we'll look at endings where one side has a Rook and a lone pawn, while the other side is defending with just a Rook. These are tricky endgames, but when you learn the examples in this chapter, you'll handle them better than almost anyone you play against, and you'll find yourself turning draws into wins and losses into draws.

The basic idea is this: The defender wants to get his King in front of the advancing pawn. If he can do that, he'll mostly get his draw. The winning side tries to use his Rook to keep the defender's King cut off from the pawn, either along a file or a rank. If the defender's King can't get to the pawn, he'll mostly lose.

These endings require a surgeon's touch, so study these examples closely.

DEFENDER'S KING IN FRONT OF THE PAWN
If you can get your King in front of the enemy pawn, you should be able to draw the game by playing alertly. Let's see just how it's done.

Diagram 8: White on Move

Black's pawn is marching down the g-file, but White's King has managed to reach the Queening square, g1. Can Black force the pawn through? Not if White knows what he's doing.

Here's how White should play to secure the draw:

    1   Rb8-b3!

This is the critical idea. White's Rook guards the third rank, making it impossible for Black to move his King there. If Black does nothing, White just shuffles his Rook along the third rank, holding his position.

What can Black do? He could try checking:

1	...	Ra2-a1 check
2	Kg1-g2	Ra1-a2 check
3	Kg2-g1	

Well, that didn't accomplish much. If he moves his Rook along the second rank, White just moves his Rook along the third:

3	...	Ra2-c2
4	Rb3-a3	Rc2-b2
5	Ra3-c3	

This isn't going anywhere. The only serious try is to push the pawn.

| 5 | ... | g4-g3 |

Diagram 9: White on Move

Now Black has a real threat. He plans to play Kh4-h3 and Rb2-b1 checkmate. Can you see how to stop this plan?

| 6 | Rc3-c8! | |

This is the other half of White's idea. When Black advances his pawn to the third rank, White moves his Rook back to the eighth, and starts giving checks. Because Black's pawn is occupying a key square on the third rank, he won't have anyplace to hide from the checks.

6	...	Kh4-h3
7	Rc8-h8 check!	Kh3-g4
8	Rh8-g8 check	Kg4-f3
9	Rg8-f8 check	Kf3-e4
10	Rf8-e8 check	

Where can Black's King go? There's no hiding spot from the checks. If the King goes back toward the pawn, White just keeps checking. If he tries to run back toward the Rook —

| 10 | ... | Ke4-d5 |
| 11 | Re8-g8! | |

White just stops the checks and goes back to capture the undefended pawn.

| 11 | ... | Rb2-b3 |
| 12 | Kg1-g2! | |

Next turn White captures the pawn with his Rook and the game is a draw.

White started out controlling the third rank with his Rook to prevent Black from moving his King there, creating checkmating threats. Once Black was forced to put his pawn on the third rank, he had no hiding places from the checks.

DEFENDER'S KING IS CUT OFF

If you're the player with the extra pawn, and you can stop your opponent's King from getting in front of your pawn, you'll probably be able to win. Take a look at the next position, and I'll show you the right way to play:

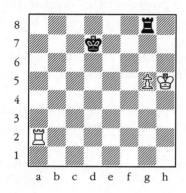

Diagram 10: Black on Move

White's got an extra pawn in Diagram 10. Black's going to try and block the pawn with his King.

> 1   ...   Kd7-e7

The King heads for f7 and g7, blocking the pawn. What should White do? There's only one good move.

> 2   Ra2-f2!

This is it! The Rook takes up position on the f-file, cutting off the Black King. Now the Black King can never reach g8, so Black will have to stop the pawn with his Rook. That's much more difficult.

> 2   ...   Rg8-h8 check

White was threatening to play Kh5-h6 and g5-g6. Black tries to keep White from moving his pawn by checking the King.

> 3   Kh5-g6!

The White King blocks the pawn, but this is just temporary. White has a two-stage plan to win:

First, use the King to push the Black Rook out of the way. This will allow White to get his King to g8 and his pawn to g7.

Second, use his Rook to help extricate the King from in front of the pawn, allowing the pawn to push through to Queen.

Black can't stop this plan, although he can make things difficult for White. Let's see how play would proceed.

> 3   ...   Rh8-g8 check

Black keeps checking.

> 4   Kg6-h6

White can't play Kg6-h7, because Black would then take White's pawn. The King and pawn have to work together.

> 4   ...   Rg8-h8 check
> 5   Kh6-g7!

The decisive move for this part of the plan. The King grabs control of the squares in front of the pawn, forcing the Black Rook to run away.

Diagram 11: Black on Move

| 5 | ... | Rh8-h1 |

The Rook can't stay in front of the pawn any longer. Instead he moves behind the pawn, and tries to annoy White by checking from the rear.

It's now easy for White to get his pawn to the seventh rank with his King in front of it. The next few moves go like this:

| 6 | g5-g6 | Rh1-h3 |

There's no point in moving the Black King. Actually it's doing a good job where it is, guarding the squares f6, f7, and f8, and preventing the White King from moving in that direction.

| 7 | Kg7-g8 | Rh3-h1 |
| 8 | g6-g7 | Rh1-h3 |

Diagram 12: White on Move

Now what? White's King is blocked from moving by the Black Rook and the Black King, and White's pawn can't advance until the King can extricate itself somehow. The next part of the plan is up to the Rook.

| 9 | Rf2-f4! |

This is the key move for White. What he's doing is called "building a bridge". By putting the Rook on the fourth rank, he'll be able to use it to block a check in a few moves.

> 9   ...   Rh3-h1

Black can only await developments.

> 10   Rf4-e4 check!

This is the other key move. Up to now the Rook has held its position on the f-file to keep the Black King cut off from the pawn. With the pawn on the seventh rank, however, White can actually let the King approach if he wishes.

Diagram 13: Black is in Check

> 10   ...   Ke7-d7

Black would like to move over and attack the pawn, but that allows White a very easy win since the Black King himself blocks the f-file. After 10 ... Ke7-f6, White just plays 11 Kg8-f8! and his pawn Queens next turn. Instead, Black has to move one more file away from the pawn. But now the King doesn't control f7 any longer, so the White King can emerge from his grotto.

11	Kg8-f7!

Now White threatens to Queen the pawn, so Black needs to start checking.

11	...	Rh1-f1 check
12	Kf7-g6	Rf1-g1 check
13	Kg6-f6	Rg1-f1 check
14	Kf6-g5	

Can White ever get away from these checks?

14	...	Rf1-g1 check

Diagram 14: White on Move

15	Re4-g4!

Yes, indeed! Now we can see why White put the Rook on the fourth rank back on his ninth move. He's able to use it as a blocker to stop the checks. Since Black can't prevent White from Queening his pawn next turn, he gives up.

This is a key endgame, so play through it a few times and make sure you understand White's entire maneuver.

White can run into some problems if his pawn is very far back. Take a look at the next position:

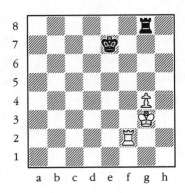

Diagram 15: White on Move

This looks a lot like the previous problem. Black's King is cut off from the pawn by the White Rook at f2. Black's Rook stops the White pawn for now, but the White King is ready to assist its advance.

However, it's crucially different in one respect: the White pawn is only on the fourth rank, not the fifth as before. Believe it or not, that small difference allows Black to draw the game. Watch what happens when White tries to advance his pawn.

1	Kg3-h4	Rg8-h8 check
2	Kh4-g5	

As before, the White King moves in front of its pawn to try and clear the way.

2	...	Rh8-g8 check
3	Kg5-h5	Rg8-h8 check
4	Kh5-g6	Rh8-g8 check

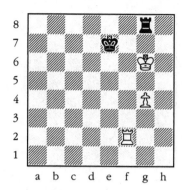

Diagram 16: White on Move

Notice the problem. If White continues to push his King forward, he loses the pawn behind it. The only way White can keep his pawn is to retreat by Kg6-h5, but then Black just keeps checking forever. That extra rank between the White pawn and the Black Rook gave Black just enough space to let him keep checking at a safe distance.

DEFENDER'S KING CUT OFF BY THREE FILES

White can win some positions with a pawn on the fourth rank, but in order to do so, the Black King has to be cut off by at least three files. The reason is that White will need to use his Rook to help advance the pawn (the last example showed why the King can't do this alone) and while the Rook is helping, the Black King will creep closer. The White Rook has to help the pawn but still have time to keep the Black King at least one file away at the end.

The next position shows the idea:

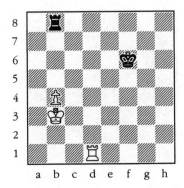

Diagram 17: White on Move

Knowing he has to buy himself some time later on, White starts by keeping the enemy King as far away as possible.

      1   Rd1-e1!

Now the Black King is a full three files away from the White pawn.

      1   ...   Kf6-f5

Black's Rook is currently on the best possible square, where it stops the pawn from as great a distance as possible. A move like 1 ... Rb8-b7?, which shortens the distance between the White pawn and the Black Rook, just makes White's job easier.

      2   Kb3-c4

With the enemy King cut off, the White King makes its move up the board.

      2   ...   Rb8-c8 check

Black starts his delaying checks.

3   Kc4-d5!

White steps to the center, away from his own pawn. In the previous position, White didn't have this option because the Black King was too close.

3   ...   Rc8-b8

There's no point in further checks, because the White King will just continue to advance. (There's no pawn behind the King for White to be concerned about.) Instead, Black just returns to attacking the pawn. If White retreats with 4 Kd5-c5, Black can start checking again.

4   Re1-b1!

Not this time! The Rook lifts its blockade of the Black King to help push the pawn forward.

4   ...   Kf5-f6

The Rook can't stop the pawn by itself. If Black plays 4 ... Rb8-b5 check, White has 5 Kd5-c6, and the pawn moves next turn.

5	b4-b5	Kf6-e7
6	Kd5-c6!	

White's careful not to get outflanked. If he blindly played 6 b5-b6, Black would move 6 ... Ke7-d7, and his King would get in front of the pawn.

6	...	Ke7-d8
7	b5-b6	Kd8-c8

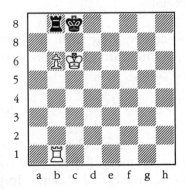

Diagram 18: White on Move

The King got in front of the pawn, but the cost was too high: Black's Rook is immobilized.

> 8   Rb1-h1!

The threat is 9 Rh1-h8 checkmate, and Black can't do much about it.

CUTTING OFF THE DEFENDER ON THE RANK

There's another way for White to win these endings besides keeping the Black King cut off on one side of the board. It's also possible to isolate Black's King on a rank, so that the problem of guarding the Queening square falls entirely on the Black Rook. This method can only be tried if the Black King has penetrated deeply into White's half of the board which makes it less common than the approach we've seen so far. Take a look at position 19:

Diagram 19: White on Move

White's pawn is only on the second rank. We now know that's not good for White's winning chances. If White tries to cut the King off by playing 1 Rh7-d7, the Black King will still be close enough to secure an eventual draw.

However, White has another plan of attack. Black's King has wandered far into enemy territory. Watch how White takes advantage of this.

    1   Rh7-h4!

White moves the Rook back and seizes control of the fourth rank. Now the Black King is confined to the box of squares from d3 to h1. Once White gets his pawn marching, the King won't be able to get anywhere close to the b8 square.

    1   ...   Ke3-d3

The King tries to stay as close to the White pawn as possible.

    2   Rh4-a4!

This is the second part of White's maneuver. By moving to a4, the Rook creates a little pocket of safety for the King to move off the first rank. If White didn't make this play, the Black Rook would just keep checking the King as soon as it emerged from b1.

| | 2 | ... | Rb8-h8 |

Black can't stop the King from escaping, so he'll try to pin the pawn on b2.

| | 3 | Kb1-a2 | Rh8-h2 |

Pins the pawn and prevents it from advancing.

| | 4 | Ra4-g4 | |

White keeps the Rook on the fourth rank, but moves it away from a4 so the King can advance along with the pawn.

| | 4 | ... | Rh2-f2 |
| | 5 | Ka2-a3 | |

This step unpins the pawn on b2, which is now free to move to b8.

| | 5 | ... | Rf2-f1 |
| | 6 | b2-b4 | Kd3-c3 |

The Black King gets closer, but it's still cut off by the White Rook. Right now, however, Black has a threat: Rf1-a1 checkmate!

| | 7 | Ka3-a4 | |

White sidesteps the threat and keeps the King and pawn moving forward.

| | 7 | ... | Rf1-a1 check |
| | 8 | Ka4-b5 | Ra1-a8 |

The Rook is useless behind the pawn, so it moves back in front. But without the help of the Black King, the Rook can't do much.

9	Rg4-g3 check	

This chases the Black King away from attacking the pawn.

9	...	Kc3-d4
10	Kb5-c6!	

White reaches a key square, where he both blocks out the Black King, assists his pawn, and chases away the Black Rook.

10	...	Ra8-c8 check
11	Kc6-b7	Rc8-c1
12	b4-b5	Kd4-c5
13	b5-b6	Rc1-b1
14	Rg3-g6!	

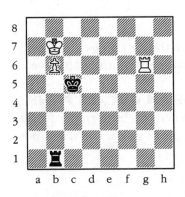

Diagram 20: Black on Move

The Rook move is the final stroke. The pawn is now protected, and the Black King is still cut off, this time on the sixth rank. The pawn will march on to b8 and the Rook won't be able to stop it.

6. ROOK & PAWNS AGAINST ROOK & PAWNS

When Rook and pawns battle against Rook and pawns, one feature dominates the game — an active Rook. If your Rook is active (attacking enemy pawns, pushing your passed pawns up the board, and restricting the enemy King) you'll have real chances to win, even if you don't have any extra pawns.

If your Rook is passively defending, you're in real trouble. It's going to be hard to win, even if you are a pawn ahead, and you may even lose.

Your top priority in these endings is simple: Activate your Rook, and keep your opponent on the defensive!

THE POWER OF AN OUTSIDE PAWN

When there are pawns on both sides of the board and you have an extra pawn, in most cases, you'll be able to win the game if you play well.

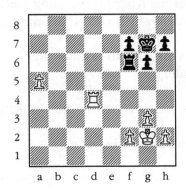

Diagram 21: Black on Move

Position 21 is taken from the 34th match game between Alexander Alekhine and Jose Capablanca in 1927. Capablanca had been World Champion in 1927. In this dramatic game, he lost the title to Alekhine, who went on to hold the title (with one brief interruption) until his death in 1946.

In the position, Alekhine has an extra passed pawn on the a-file. In addition, his Rook is very well placed, able to get to a4 behind his pawn and push it up the board. In an ending like this, you're a lot better off if you can guard your pawn from the rear (squares like a4, a3, a2, or a1) than from the side (d5) or the front (a8 or a7). Once your Rook is behind the pawn, your opponent has to physically block the pawn by putting one of his pieces (probably the Rook) in front of it. As your pawn goes farther up the board, the scope of your Rook increases and the scope of your opponent's Rook decreases. That's good for you.

What is Alekhine's winning plan? Basically, it consists of six steps:

(1) Put his Rook behind his pawn — very important. Black will then have to block the a-pawn with his Rook.

(2) Move his King to the center of the board.

(3) If Black leaves his King on the King's side of the board, attack the Black Rook which will be stopping the a-pawn.

(4) If Black moves the King to assist his Rook, attack the pawns left on the Kingside.

(5) Sacrifice the a-pawn to capture Black's King-side pawns.

(6) Queen a pawn on the King-side.

Let's watch while Alekhine puts the plan into practice.

	1	...	Rf6-a6

Blocking the pawn. Black would be forced to this position next turn anyway.

	2	Rd4-a4

Puts the Rook in the right place. 2 Rd4-d5 would also win, but with more effort. Part one of the plan is complete.

	2	...	Kg7-f6

Black's King emerges to contest the center of the board.

	3	Kg2-f3	Kf6-e5

Black's King reaches the center first.

	4	Kf3-e3

White has also centralized, so part two of his plan is complete. Will he be able to penetrate on one side of the board or the other, or will Black's King somehow be able to oppose him? That's the question for the next phase of the game.

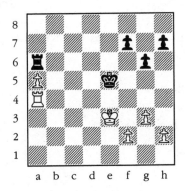

Diagram 22: Black to Move

4   ...   h7-h5

Black really doesn't want to move his King-side pawns. The more he moves them, the closer they get to White's King and the easier they become to attack. Unfortunately, Black doesn't have a lot of choice.

If Black moves his Rook (4 ... Ra6-a7), White just pushes his pawn closer to Queening with 5 a5-a6.

If Black moves his King to the left, 4 ... Ke5-d5, White sidesteps to the right (5 Ke3-f4) and starts to penetrate the King's-side.

If Black moves his King to the right, 4 ... Ke5-f5, White side-steps to the left (5 Ke3-d4) and goes after the Black Rook.

So Black's best chance is to leave his pieces in their current, optimal positions and try to fiddle with his pawns hoping that the weaknesses he creates won't be too damaging.

5   Ke3-d3

Alekhine threatens to move on the Rook with K-c4-b5.

| 5 | ... | Ke5-d5 |

Black blocks that plan and keeps the Kings opposed. Can he maintain the blockade?

| 6 | Kd3-c3 |

Again White tries to sidestep.

| 6 | ... | Kd5-c5 |

And again Black takes up a blockading position.

| 7 | Ra4-a2! |

This is what's called a tempo move. White simply makes a meaningless move with his Rook to throw the onus of moving onto Black. As we saw before, Black's Rook can't move without letting the pawn advance, while a King move to either side allows White to penetrate on the other side.

| 7 | ... | Kc5-b5 |

Black decides that his best chance is to try and eliminate the pawn.

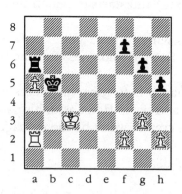

Diagram 23: White on Move

8   Kc3-d4!

White sidesteps to the right and heads for the Kingside. He can't protect his pawn anymore and he doesn't have to.

What both players now see is that if Black takes the White pawn, his King will be left too far out of play to stop White's attack on the King-side. After 8 ... Ra6xa5 9 Ra2xa5 check Kb5xa5, White just plays 10 Kd4-e5, followed by moving the King to f6 and capturing the pawn on f7. After that, it's just a matter of Queening one of his own pawns.

8   ...   Ra6-d6 check!

Black puts up a good fight. His plan is to move the Rook away with check, then push his King into a6. That way his King will stop the pawn while his Rook guards the King-side. It's a clever idea, one that just might work.

9   Kd4-e5   Rd6-e6 check

Black checks again from a square where the Rook is guarded. He'll move the King into a6 next turn.

10   Ke5-f4

White is still planning on attacking the King-side with his King.

10   ...   Kb5-a6

Black has successfully switched defenders. Now he has to wait and see what White tries next.

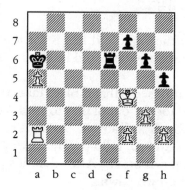

Diagram 24: White on Move

| 11 | Kf4-g5 |

The penetration starts. White is headed for g7 via h6.

| 11 | ... | Re6-e5 check |

Black can't stop White from reaching g7, so he has to try to set up a defensive formation once White gets there. This check helps him reposition his Rook at f5. From that square, he can safely guard his pawn at f7, the critical weak link in his pawn chain. (The other pawns are all guarded by pawns, so they're safe from an attack by pieces.)

| 12 | Kg5-h6 | Re5-f5 |
| 13 | f2-f4 | |

Now White threatens 14 h2-h4 followed by 15 Kh6-g7, after which Black will be completely out of playable moves.

| 13 | ... | Rf5-d5! |

Black repositions the Rook to guard the f7-pawn from d7. That way, the Rook will have different squares to move to while still defending the pawn.

| 14 | Kh6-g7 | Rd5-d7 |

Can Black hold this new defensive position?

| 15 | Kg7-f6 | Rd7-c7 |

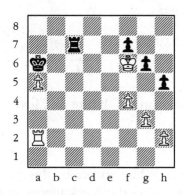

Diagram 25: White on Move

Is White stymied, or is there a new way to break through?

| 16 | f4-f5! |

The pawn leads the way. This move breaks up Black's pawn chain and makes the h-pawn easier to attack.

| 16 | ... | g6xf5 |

Allowing White to capture on g6 isn't an improvement. If Black tries 16 ... Rc7-c6 check 17 Kf6xf7 g6xf5, White wins the King-side pawns with 18 Ra2-f2!

| 17 | Kf6xf5 |

Now the pawn on h5 is vulnerable to attack.

| 17 | ... | Rc7-c5 check |
| 18 | Kf5-f6 | Rc5-c7 |

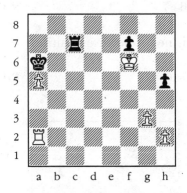

Diagram 26: White on Move

19	Ra2-f2!	

This is the key idea. White abandons the a-pawn, which has done its job by distracting the Black pieces, and concentrates all his firepower on the King-side pawns.

19	...	Ka6xa5

Black has nothing better.

20	Rf2-f5 check	Ka5-b6
21	Rf5xh5	Kb6-c6

Black's King heads for the King-side as fast as possible...

22	Rh5-h7

... but it's too late. White wins the f7-pawn as well.

22	...	Kc6-d6
23	Rh7xf7	

With two extra pawns, White will win the ending pretty easily although it will still take a few more moves.

THE ACTIVE ROOK

As we said at the beginning of this chapter, in Rook and pawn endings the most important principle is to keep your pieces active. In many, if not most positions, active, well-placed pieces are more important than being a pawn ahead.

The next position shows this principle in action. The player of the Black pieces, the great endgame artist Akiba Rubinstein, passes up many opportunities to win a quick pawn, trying instead to see that his Rook and King remain actively placed. Eventually, when he feels he has a secure grip on the position, he carefully harvests his opponent's weak pawns.

Diagram 27: Black on Move

At first glance, White might appear to be doing well in Position 27. He has an outside passed pawn, on the a-file, and his Rook can get behind the pawn, on the a2-square, and push it up the board.

In fact, if Black tries to win a pawn right away, he could easily get into trouble. Suppose he plays 1 ... Rb8-b3 (attacking the a-pawn) 2 Rc2-a2 Rb3-d3 (winning the d-pawn). White would ignore the attack on the d-pawn and just start pushing his passed pawn: 3 a3-a4! Rd3xd4 4 a4-a5 Rd4-c4 (to try to block the passed pawn) 5 a5-a6! Rc4-c8 6 a6-a7 Rc8-a8. Black would then be completely tied down, and White certainly wouldn't lose the position.

In Rook and pawn endings, a good player avoids variations where his pieces become passive defenders. The winning idea is to make your own pieces active, while your opponent's pieces become passive. Rubinstein probably didn't spend more than a few seconds discarding the previous variation. Let's see how he decided to handle the game:

1 ... Rb8-a8!

Black attacks the pawn at a3.

2 Rc2-c3

White protects the pawn and keeps his Rook free to maneuver along the third rank.

2 ... Ra8-a4!

Very good. Rubinstein stops the pawn dead in its tracks, while simultaneously attacking the pawn on d4.

Notice that this simple maneuver (R-a8-a4) has already given Black an active and aggressive Rook, while White's Rook is stuck in a defensive role guarding the a-pawn.

3 Rc3-d3

The Rook guards the d-pawn, but already White is in trouble. His Rook is guarding pawns, Black's Rook is attacking them.

3 ... Kf8-e7

Black's next job is to relocate the King to its best square, in this case, d5, where it attacks the pawn on d4 and threatens to penetrate the White position at either c4 or e4.

4 Kh2-g3

White tries to centralize his King as well.

4	...	Ke7-e6
5	Kg3-f3	Ke6-d5

Black reaches the center first. Now White has to worry about losing his d-pawn at some point.

6	Kf3-e2!

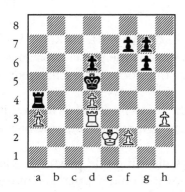

Diagram 28: Black on Move

White gets to make good moves too! In this case White sets a subtle trap. Apparently Black can now just capture the pawn on d4 leaving himself a pawn ahead, but that's actually a bad mistake. If Black plays 6 ... Ra4xd4, White responds with 7 Ke2-e3! Rd4xd3 check 8 Ke3xd3. Now White will use his passed pawn on the a-file as a decoy forcing the Black King over to the edge of the board to stop it. Meanwhile the White King will move up the d-file capturing the pawn at d6 and then moving among the Black pawns on the Kingside. Black might save a draw, but it would be very difficult.

Rubinstein sees through this trap and refuses to fall for the bait. Instead he improves his position, gradually depriving White of moves.

6	...	g6-g5!

Now the White pawn at h3 can't move.

> 7   Rd3-b3

White doesn't want to be stuck in a passive position forever. The idea of this move is to get behind the Black pawns, trying to exchange as many as possible.

> 7   ...   f7-f6!

If Black captured the d-pawn with his Rook, White would play 8 Rb3-d3! and again the outside passed a-pawn would give White a strong game after the Rooks get exchanged.

If Black captures the d-pawn with his King, White plays Rb3-b7, and he'll pick off enough of the King-side pawns to get a draw.

Instead Black puts his King-side pawns on easily defendable squares, and here's what could happen if White goes after them: 8 Rb3-b7 Ra4xa3 9 Rb7xg7 Ra3xh3. Black will eventually win the d-pawn as well, leaving him two pawns ahead.

> 8   Ke2-e3

White now realizes his plan won't work, so he settles down to a defensive position. His big problem is that all his pawns are isolated, so they must all be defended by pieces — a cumbersome task.

> 8   ...   Kd5-c4

Black keeps grabbing more space. The more active your pieces are, the more space they can eventually bring under their control.

> 9   Rb3-d3

The only square for the Rook if White doesn't want to lose his a-pawn and h-pawn. But now White's pieces are starting to run out of squares. The Rook has no moves, and the King has to stay where it protects the Rook.

9	...	d6-d5!

Takes the square e4 away from the White King.

10	Ke3-d2

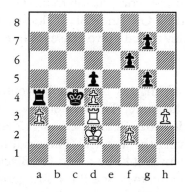

Diagram 29 Black on Move

10	...	Ra4-a8!

An excellent repositioning move. The Rook has done its job at a4. Now that Black's King controls the Queenside, the Rook seeks out more activity. Black's main idea is to invade along the b-file, as in this variation: 11 Kd2-e3 Ra8-b8 12 Ke3-d2 Rb8-b2 check 13 Kd2-e3 Rb2-a2, and White is just about out of moves.

11	Kd2-c2

Temporarily stops that idea.

11	...	Ra8-a7!

Black waits until White moves his King back to d2.

     12   Kc2-d2

White can't move his Rook anywhere without losing either the d-pawn or the a-pawn, and this is the only square where the King can guard the Rook.

     12   ...   Ra7-e7!

This move puts White into a situation known as zugswang — a German word meaning "compulsion to move." If White didn't have to move, he'd be OK since Black doesn't actually have a threat. However, any actual move causes White to lose in some way.

If White keeps shuffling his King, he'll eventually lose his a-pawn, and with it the game. The sequence would be 13 Kd2-c2 Re7-e2 check 14 Rd3-d2 Re2xd2 check 15 Kc2xd2 Kc4-b3! followed by capturing the a-pawn. The resulting ending with just Kings and pawns would be a win for Black. (For tips on how to win these endgames, see Basic Endgame Strategy, volume 1 in the "Road to Chess Mastery" series.)

     13   Rd3-c3 check

White realizes he can't hold on to everything, so he abandons the d-pawn to get some activity for his Rook.

     13   ...   Kc4xd4

Black records his first profit for his fine maneuvering.

     14   a3-a4!

White uses his best asset, the passed a-pawn. With his Rook behind it on a3, this could become a powerful force.

| 14 | ... | Re7-a7 |
| 15 | Rc3-a3 | Ra7-a5! |

Black blockades the pawn as quickly as possible.

| 16 | Ra3-a1 | |

Although White has a passed pawn, there's no way to advance it, so he begins shuttling his Rook between a3 and a1.

16	...	Kd4-c4
17	Kd2-e3	d5-d4 check
18	Ke3-d2	

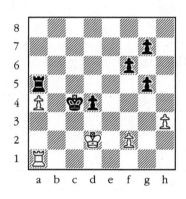

Diagram 30: Black on Move

Black's made as much progress as he can with the current arrangement of pieces. In these endings, when your opponent has managed to block your progress, the way to move forward is to open up a new front.

| 18 | ... | Ra5-f5! |

The right idea. Black goes after the weak f-pawn, which White left undefended when he tried to block Black's progress on the Queenside. Black has calculated exactly — he'll just have time to pick off the f-pawn and get back in time to stop the a-pawn.

19	Kd2-e1

An abject retreat, but White saw that Black had calculated correctly. If White pushed his a-pawn, this is what would have happened: 19 a4-a5 Rf5xf2 check 20 Kd2-e1 Rf2-b2 21 a5-a6 Rb2-b8 22 a6-a7 Rb8-a8, arriving just in time. Black would then move his King back, Kc4-c5-b6, and capture the a-pawn with his Rook.

19	...	Kc4-b4

Just as we saw in the previous ending: Black is switching block-aders, to free his Rook to attack the f-pawn and h-pawn.

20	Ke1-e2	Kb4-a4

The pawn is securely blocked and the Rook is free. If White's Rook ever leaves the a-file, the King will capture the pawn.

21	Ra1-a3	Rf5-f4

A good square for the Rook. It guards the d-pawn while still attacking the White pawns.

22	Ra3-a2

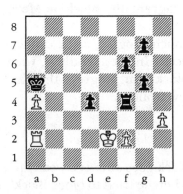

Diagram 31: Black on Move

| 22 | ... | Rf4-h4! |

Black goes after the h-pawn. If White tries to defend it with 23 Ra2-a3, Black plays 23 ... Ka5-b4! and the Rook can no longer defend both the a-pawn and the h-pawn. That's an example of the tactical theme called "The Overworked Piece", explained in detail in Winning Chess Tactics, part of the "Road to Chess Mastery" series.

| 23 | Ke2-d3 | Rh4xh3 check |
| 24 | Kd3xd4 | Rh3-h4 check! |

Another tactical theme, this time the Skewer. Black checks the King and wins the a-pawn, located behind the King on the same line.

| 25 | Kd4-d3 | Rh4xa4 |

Black is now two pawns ahead, and White's King is cut off from the Black pawns. From this point on, the win is pretty easy.

| 26 | Ra2-e2 | |

If White exchanges Rooks he has no chance. From e2, the Rook is hoping to reach e7 or e8, where it may cause some trouble among the Black pawns.

| 26 | ... | Ra4-f4! |

Ties the White Rook down to guarding the f-pawn.

| 27 | Kd3-e3 | |

The King takes over the job of guarding the f-pawn, freeing the Rook for further action. Although White should lose this ending now, he's still going to try to put up stiff resistance. A tactical trick or two may well appear, and if Black relaxes his attention, White might still save the game.

27	...	Ka5-b6

Diagram 32: White on Move

28	Re2-c2!	

White keeps fighting. This move cuts the Black King off from the King-side.

28	...	Kb6-b7

The White Rook could become a nuisance if White were allowed to play Rc2-c8-g8, getting behind the Black pawns. The King move keeps the Rook out.

29	Rc2-c1	

White temporizes, waiting for Black to try something. The upside to White's losing his pawns is that his pieces don't have much to protect anymore, so now they're free to roam around!

29	...	Rf4-a4

The Rook can't do much from f4. One idea is to move it to c8 via a8, enabling the King to cross over to the Kingside.

30	Rc1-h1	

Threatening to win a pawn by Rh1-h7 and Rxg7.

| 30 | ... | Kb7-c6 |

Opens up the seventh rank. Black can now respond to Rh1-h7 with Ra4-a7.

| 31 | Rh1-h7 | Ra4-a7 |
| 32 | Ke3-e4 | Kc6-d6 |

The King will take over the job of defending the pawns.

| 33 | Ke4-f5 | |

White overlooks a tactical shot which finishes the game. If White had stayed back with his King, Black would still have won by advancing his pawns, but it would have been a slow process.

| 33 | ... | g7-g6 check! |

Attacks the King and uncovers an attack on the Rook.

| 34 | Kf5xg6 | Ra7xh7 |
| 35 | Kg6xh7 | Kd6-e5! |

The Black King moves in on the last White pawn. The White King is caught offside.

| 36 | Kh7-g6 | g5-g4! |

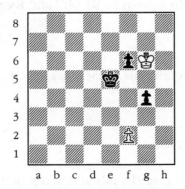

Diagram 33: White Resigns

White can't stop Black from eventually Queening a pawn.

7. QUEEN AGAINST PAWN

Queen against pawn? Doesn't that sound like a pretty big mismatch? What chance can a lowly pawn have against a powerful Queen?

In most cases, not much. But in a few cases, the side with the pawn can actually fight the mighty Queen to a draw. Let's look at how this can be done, and perhaps you'll be able to pull out an amazing save in one of your own games!

WINNING AGAINST A PAWN THAT'S TOO FAR BACK

Diagram 34: White on Move

The first point to notice about these endings is that unless the pawn has advanced to its seventh rank, one square away from Queening) it doesn't have much of a chance. Diagram 34 shows why. Although White's King and Queen couldn't be farther away, and the pawn is already on its sixth row, White stops it easily.

| 1 | Qh8-h1! | a3-a2 |
| 2 | Qh1-a1! | |

That's it. Once the Queen gets in front of the pawn, she just sits there until White brings up the King, and then White's two pieces will force Black's King away from the pawn.

| 2 | ... | Kb4-b3 |
| 3 | Kg7-f6 | Kb3-a3 |

To avoid losing the pawn, Black's King has to shuttle between b3 and a3. Meanwhile White closes in for the kill.

4	Kf6-e5	Ka3-b3
5	Ke5-d4	Kb3-a3
6	Kd4-c4!	

The quickest finish.

| 6 | ... | Ka3-a4 |
| 7 | Qa1xa2 checkmate | |

If the pawn is already on the seventh rank, ready to Queen, the other side has more problems. Take a look at the next position.

WINNING AGAINST A CENTER PAWN

Diagram 35: White on Move

White can still win here, but it's not as easy as in the last example. First he has to gain time for his King to approach.

1	Qg8-c4 check	Kc2-b2

Black threatens to Queen the pawn again.

2	Qc4-d3!	

White attacks the pawn and also prevents Queening.

2	...	Kb2-c1

Black guards the pawn and again threatens to Queen.

3	Qd3-c3 check!	

This is the key move. To save his pawn, Black has to block it with his King.

3	...	Kc1-d1
4	Kg6-f5	

When the pawn is blocked, White uses the time to bring his King closer.

| 4 | ... | Kd1-e2 |

Black emerges on the other side and again threatens to Queen.

| 5 | Qc3-c2! | |

Now White pins the pawn against the King.

| 5 | ... | Ke2-e1 |

The only move to save the pawn.

| 6 | Qc2-e4 check | |

White executes the same maneuver as before to push the Black King in front of the pawn.

6	...	Ke1-f2
7	Qe4-d3	Kf2-e1
8	Qd3-e3 check	Ke1-d1
9	Kf5-e4	

White closes in.

9	...	Kd1-c2
10	Qe3-d3 check	Kc2-c1
11	Qd3-c3 check	Kc1-d1

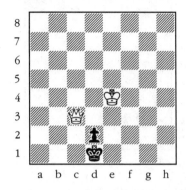

Diagram 36: White on Move

With White's King closing in, he has a checkmate in three moves.

12	Ke4-e3	Kd1-e1
13	Qc3xd2 check	Ke1-f1
14	Qd2-f2 checkmate	

DRAWING AGAINST A BISHOP'S PAWN
Does this line of play mean that you can always win against a pawn on the seventh rank? Surprisingly the answer is no. The method you've just learned works perfectly well if the pawn is on the King file (e-file), the Queen file (d-file), or either Knight file (b-file or g-file). But if the pawn is on one of the Bishop's files (c-file or f-file), it won't work if the defender knows a tactical trick!

Take a look at the next position:

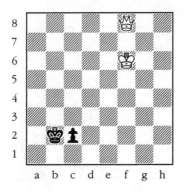

Diagram 37: White on Move

This is the same as position 35, but all the pieces have moved one file to the left. Now the Black pawn is on the c-file, and this means Black can draw the game if he knows how. Let's watch how the play develops.

> 1 Qf8-b4 check

White starts as before. He wants to push the Black King in front of the pawn so his own King can approach.

1	...	Kb2-a2
2	Qb4-c3	Ka2-b1
3	Qc3-b3 check	

Diagram 38: Black on Move

So far so good. Now White expects the Black King to move to c1, and he'll use the next move to bring his own King closer. But look what Black has in mind.

> 3   ...   Kb1-a1!

Black doesn't protect the pawn at all! He just sticks his King in the corner, and if White plays 4 Qb3xc2, it's a stalemate!

White is stuck. He has to keep checking, and can't ever gain a move to bring up his King. The game is a draw.

The side with the pawn isn't the only side with tactical tricks in these endings. If White's King is close enough to the scene of the action, he can win against a Bishop pawn, provided his Queen is also in the right place. Take a look at the next diagram.

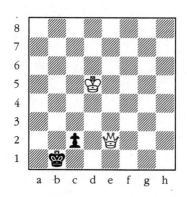

Diagram 39: White to Move can Force a Win

Black is threatening to Queen his pawn. White's response — Go right ahead!

> 1   Kd5-c4!

White actually allows Black to Queen with check!

1   ...   c2-c1 (Q) check

"It's a draw now," thinks Black.

2   Kc4-b3!

All of a sudden Black is short of good moves. White's threat is Qe2-a2 checkmate. If Black checks on b2 or c2, White just captures with his Queen. If Black moves his Queen anywhere else, White plays Qe2-b2 checkmate. Black got his Queen, but it wasn't enough to stop checkmate.

If Black has a Rook's pawn (a-file or h-file) on the seventh rank against a Queen, that's also a draw. When White maneuvers to force the Black King in front of the pawn, Black ends up stalemated. Again, White won't have time to advance his own King.

8. QUEEN & PAWN AGAINST QUEEN

Endings where a Queen and pawn try to defeat a lone Queen are especially tricky, and cause problems for even the best players. The defender has plenty of chances to draw the game, with a powerful Queen roaming the board and ready to give check at every turn.

There are a few simple rules, however, which will allow you to play these endings pretty well. If you know them, you'll be way ahead of your opponents, and you'll be able to save many a lost game, or turn a theoretically drawn game into a win.

DEFENDER IN FRONT OF THE PAWN

The first rule is an easy one, very similar to the situation in Rook endings. If the defender's King can block the pawn, the game should be a draw. Take a look at Position 40:

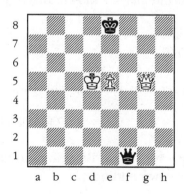

Diagram 40: Black on Move

White has a pawn on the e-file, but Black has managed to get his King to e8, a square in front of the pawn. Now Black can draw the game pretty simply, just by checking with his Queen. Here's how the play might go.

| 1 | ... | Qf1-b5 check |

Black's plan is just to annoy the King with a lot of checks. Some-times he can even set a trap or two.

| 2 | Kd5-e4 | |

Did you see the trap? If White played the apparently aggressive 2 Kd5-e6??, Black could checkmate him in two moves! 2 ... Qb5-d7 check 3 Ke6-f6 (forced) Qd7-f7 checkmate! The Queen can be a very powerful defender indeed!

| 2 | ... | Qb5-c4 check |
| 3 | Ke4-f5 | |

Black had another trap: If White played 3 Ke4-e3, Black would play Qc4-c1 check!, winning the White Queen with a skewer.

| 3 | ... | Qc4-d3 check |

Another trap: If White plays 4 Kf5-e6, Black again checkmates after 4 ... Qd3-d7.

| 4 | Kf5-f6 | |

White is trying to get away from the checks.

| 4 | ... | Qd3-d8 check! |

This is the simplest way to draw. Black aims to exchange Queens and then draw the pawn ending.

| 5 | Kf6-g6 | Qd8xg5 check |

6	Kg6xg5	Ke8-e7!
7	Kg5-f5	Ke7-f7!

If you remember your King and pawn endings from the first volume of Basic Endgame Strategy: Kings, Pawns and Minor Pieces, you know that this endgame is a draw. (See Problem 17 in that book.)

WINNING WITH A BLOCKING CHECK

To have real winning chances in these endings, White (the side with the extra pawn) needs to get his pawn to the seventh rank. Where should Black's King be if he can't get right in front of the pawn? Amazingly, if the Black King can't actually block the pawn, he should get as far away from the pawn as possible! This is completely different from the situation in all other endings where the defending King is always trying to get as close to the passed pawns as possible.

The reason the defender's King wants to get far away is that the defender's best chances lie in creating a perpetual check with his Queen. For this to work, the defender's Queen needs to have freedom of movement around the pawn. If the King is close by, it may well get in the way.

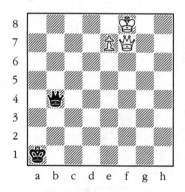

Diagram 41: White on Move

Diagram 41 shows a pretty easy win for White. Right now Black's Queen is pinning the pawn to White's King. Black's King is far away, but unfortunately it's located on a bad diagonal. Watch what happens:

> 1   Kf8-g8

Unpinning the pawn, threatening 2 e7-e8 (Q). Black has to check somewhere. But if he checks on the first rank (Qb4-b8 check), White wins by pushing his pawn. That only leaves Black a single check.

> 1 ...   Qb4-g4 check
> 2 Qf7-g7 check!

This is the standard winning idea. White tries to maneuver so he can block a check with a check, thus trading off Queens.

> 2 ...   Qg4xg7 check
> 3 Kg8xg7

...and White Queens his pawn next turn.

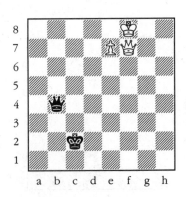

Diagram 42: White on Move

In Position 42, Black's King is on a different square, c2. White can still win, but it requires slightly more time.

     1   Kf8-g8

The first step is to unpin the pawn and threaten to advance it.

     1   ...   Qb4-g4 check

Black can't stop the pawn so he has to distract White with a check.

     2   Kg8-h8

Again threatening to push the pawn.

     2   ...   Qg4-d4 check

Black can't check on h4 or h3 because White plays Qf7-h7 check! (again blocking a check with a check) and the Queens come off the board with an easy win for White.

     3   Qf7-g7!
Stopping the checks, since 3 ... Qd4-h4 check is still answered by 4 Qg7-h7 check.

     3   ...   Qd4-d7

The only way left to stop the pawn from Queening.

     4   Qg7-g6 check!

Once again the Black King is caught on an awkward diagonal. The White Queen checks and guards e8, the Queening square. Next turn White will play e7-e8(Q), winning.

DEFEATING A WELL-PLACED KING
If the Black King is located on a good defensive square, White may not have such an easy win at his disposal. When this happens, White's best winning try is to centralize his Queen, then bring his King toward Black's King. Lining his King up with

Black's King will create more winning checks. Take a look at the next position.

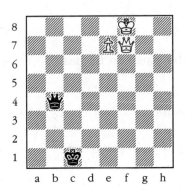

Diagram 43: White on Move

The c1 square is a great defensive square for Black's King. In the last two positions, Black's trouble came when the White Queen blocked a check on either g7 or h7. The bad squares for Black's King are squares in the lower corner of the board which are on the diagonals leading to either g7 or h7 — squares like a1, b2, c3, b1, and c2. By avoiding those squares, Black forces White to find a new winning idea.

> 1   Qf7-d5

Escaping with the King into the corner won't work in this position, as Black will just keep checking and White won't be able to block with a check. So White first centralizes his Queen (cutting down on Black's checking squares), and then prepares to move his King out.

> 1   ...   Qb4-f4 check

Black keeps checking, as usual.

> 2   Kf8-g7   Qf4-c7

Pinning the pawn is just as effective as checking.

3	Kg7-f6	Qc7-b6 check

The checks continue.

4	Kf6-f5	

In general, it's good to keep your King on squares of the opposite color of the square the Black Queen is on. This will slightly reduce the number of checks available.

4	...	Qb6-f2 check

Black only had two checks available (f2 and b1). The f2 check gives him the most options next turn.

5	Kf5-e6	

White is headed for the d, c, and b-files, where he'll have more possibilities of blocking checks with checks. Since Black's Queen is now on a dark square, White stays on white squares.

5	...	Qf2-b6 check
6	Qd5-d6	

This interposition again leaves Black with just two checks (b3 and e3).

6	...	Qb6-b3 check
7	Ke6-d7	

Diagram 44: Black on Move

Black is running out of checks. If he plays Qb3-a4 check or b5 check, White blocks with Qd6-c6 check! (Notice the power of moving the King to the same files as Black's King.)

7	...	Qb3-h3 check

The only check left.

8	Kd7-d8	Qh3-h4

With no checks left, Black must pin the pawn.

9	Qd6-d7

Covers the King.

9	...	Qh4-g5

Black has to maintain the pin.

10	Kd8-c8	Qg5-c5 check

The only check, but now ...

11	Qd7-c7!

This forces the exchange of Queens.

11	...	Qc5xc7 check
12	Kc8xc7	

White Queens his pawn next turn.

9. QUEEN & PAWNS AGAINST QUEEN & PAWNS

In endings with just Queens and pawns on the board, the winning idea is to be the first side to create a passed pawn. The combination of a passed pawn and an escorting Queen is so powerful that even an enemy Queen cannot stop the pawn by herself. Take a look at this position:

POWER OF A PASSED PAWN

Diagram 45: White on Move

White is a pawn ahead and has an outside passed pawn. If this were an ending of Bishop versus Bishop, Knight versus Knight, or Rook versus Rook, White's extra pawn would be enough to win, but the process would be long and slow, as we've seen in some previous games.

But with Queens on the board, watch what happens.

     1   a2-a4

Push the pawn!

     1   ...   Qd8-a5

Black immediately moves to blockade. Now what?

     2   Qc4-b5!

This is the key idea. White's pawn supports the Queen, and the Queen chases the Black Queen out of the way.

     2   ...   Qa5-a7

The Queen falls back to a new blockading square.

     3   a4-a5

Push the pawn!

     3   ...   Kg8-h7
     4   a5-a6!

Keep pushing!

     4   ...   g7-g5

There's not a lot that Black can do.

     5   Qb5-b7!

Once more the Queen sweeps Black out of the way.

     5   ...   Qa7-d4

Black has to move or be captured.

      6   a6-a7!

Swift and brutal. White gets a second Queen next turn.

In Diagram 45, Black simply had no chance. Accompanied by its Queen, the pawn could just race to the Queening square almost as quickly as if there were no pieces on the board at all.

DEFENDING AGAINST A PASSED PAWN

There are only two defenses to a passed pawn in a Queen ending:

(1) Another passed pawn. If both sides have passed pawns, the side whose pawn is further advanced has the advantage. It may be worth sacrificing a pawn or two just to get a passed pawn loose.

(2) Perpetual check. In the last diagram, White's King had a cozy little nest, so there was nothing Black could do. If the King's position isn't as secure, the defender may be able to organize a perpetual check.

Now let's look at some more difficult endings, where the defender has a chance of putting up a fight.

In Position 46, Black is a pawn down and White's King is very aggressively placed, but Black has a powerful passed pawn on the a-file. With good play, this is enough to win the game. Let's watch.

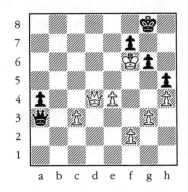

Diagram 46: Black on Move

Black's first job is to stop the threat of 1 Qd4-d8 check and 2 Kf6xf7, with mating threats.

1	...	Qa3-f8!

A fine move which accomplishes several goals in one stroke. It prevents Q-d8 check, it guards Black's King, it clears the way for the a-pawn to advance, and it indirectly guards the a-pawn itself. Do you see what happens if White now plays 2 Qd4xa4?

2	Kf6-g5

White prudently decides to retreat his King out of the danger zone. He sees that if he carelessly played 2 Qd4xa4??, Black would reply 2 ... Qf8-d6 check, and after 3 Kf6-g5 Kg8-g7! Black would have unstoppable threats of Qd6-e5 checkmate and f7-f6 checkmate.

2	...	Qf8-e7 check!

Chases the White King a little farther back while moving the Queen to a more active square.

3	Kg5-f4	a4-a3

Black has a simple plan — Queen the a-pawn. White must stop the pawn, since there's no way his own pawns can be mobilized fast enough.

4   Kf4-e3

The King is the slow-moving piece, so it has to get mobilized first. After 4 Qd4-a4 Qe7-c5! the White King might not be able to reach the Queenside.

4   ...   Qe7-b7

Prepares to go to b3 or b2 to help the pawn advance.

5   Qd4-d8 check

White has to stop the pawn as soon as possible. This check is part of a relocating maneuver, bringing the Queen to a5 via d8.

5   ...   Kg8-h7!

The right square for the King. On g7, the King would be subject to annoying checks along the d4-h8 diagonal. On h7, the only way White could give a check would be to somehow capture the f7 pawn. (Black will be very careful to see that doesn't happen.) Remember that the defender's best chance to draw is to somehow give perpetual check, so shielding your King from check is a top priority for the side trying to win.

6   Qd8-a5

Stops the pawn for the moment.

6   ...   Qb7-b2

The threat couldn't be plainer: a3-a2-a1 (Q).

7   Qa5-c7

A counter-threat: White wants to play Qc7xf7 check, followed by a perpetual check on f7 and f8.

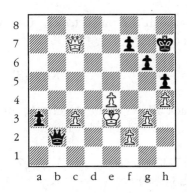

Diagram 47: Black on Move

7	...	Qb2-b3!

Black puts a stop to that nonsense. From b3 the Queen guards the key f7-square and also helps the pawn advance. In addition, it pins the c-pawn, so White can't play c3-c4, cutting off the Queen's protection of f7.

8	g2-g4

White is getting desperate. To give check, he has to somehow blast open the alleys leading to the Black King. This pawn sacrifice may help. If Black plays 8 ... h5xg4, White will try 9 h4-h5!, opening up some lines of attack.

8	...	a3-a2

Black doesn't fall for the bait, but pushes resolutely on toward a1.

9	Qc7-a5

Stops the pawn for the moment.

| 9 | ... | Qb3-b2 |

Again prepares to push the pawn to a1. Can White manufacture a perpetual check?

| 10 | Qa5-c7 | Kh7-g8! |

A clever idea. Black allows White to check, for the purpose of maneuvering his Queen to a bad square.

| 11 | Qc7-d8 check | Kg8-g7 |
| 12 | Qd8-d4 check | Kg7-h7 |

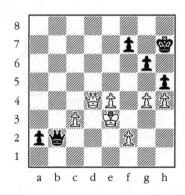

Diagram 48: White on Move

White's Queen is now at d4; it can't return to c7. That particular square is crucial because it's the only square where the White Queen performs three (!) crucial tasks: attacks f7, guards c3, and prevents the Black Queen from returning to the seventh rank herself.

| 13 | Qd4-c4 |

White does what he can. From this square the Queen threatens f7 again and still guards c3. But White has no control over the seventh rank any longer, so watch what happens.

| 13 | ... | Qb2-b6 check |

The Black Queen relocates with check.

| 14 | Ke3-e2 | Qb6-a7! |

The square Black was trying to reach. The Queen gets behind the pawn and guards f7 as well. Now the pawn can't be stopped.

| 15 | g4xh5 | |

White opens up the Kingside, but to no avail.

| 15 | ... | a2-a1(Q) |
| 16 | h5xg6 check | f7xg6 |

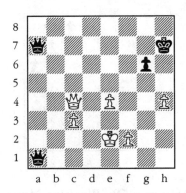

Diagram 49: White Resigns

White has no checks, and the two Queens together on an open board are overwhelming. A typical finish might be 17 h4-h5 Qa1-b2 check, and now White gets checkmated very quickly:

If 18 Ke2-d1 or e1 Qa7-a1 checkmate.

If 18 Ke2-f1 Q (either one)xf2 checkmate.

If 18 Ke2-d3 Qa7-d7 check 19 Kd3-e3 Qb2-d2 check 20 Ke3-f3 Qd7-h3 checkmate.

If 18 Ke2-f3 Qb2xf2 check 19 Kf3-g4 Qa7-d7 check with a quick mate to follow.

CREATING CHECKMATING CHANCES

If you know how to handle the Queen properly, there are winning chances in Queen endings that don't exist in other endings, because the Queen can be a powerful checkmating force all by herself.

Take a look at Diagram 50:

Diagram 50: Black on Move

Black is a pawn ahead, but all the pawns are on one side of the board. If we replaced the two Queen with two Rooks, or two Bishops, the ending would be a pretty simple draw for White. He would exchange pawns when possible, and eventually he'd block the last pawn with his King. Black then wouldn't be able to make progress.

With Queens on the board, Black concocts a different plan. He's going to boldly march his King right into the heart of enemy territory (he's headed for the f1 square!) and try to either checkmate White or force an exchange of Queens. Can White stop this simple idea? We'll see.

By the way, here's another handy rule of thumb for Queen endings: Verify that the ending with the Queens off the board is a win for you. If it is, then you can make progress by offering, or threatening, to exchange Queens. Your opponent will have to back down in each case, allowing you to carry out your plan. You'll see Black use this approach at several points in this ending.

1	...	Kg7-f6

Black's Queen is already very well-placed. It controls many center squares (cutting down on White's checks) and also guards the key pawn at f7. So Black starts the King out on his march.

2	Qd2-d8 check	

White can't improve his King's position, so he starts a series of checks.

2	...	Kf6-f5

Black boldly heads for White's territory.

3	Qd8-d7 check	

White will continue checking for as long as he can. Black still has to demonstrate that, at some point, he can avoid the checks.

3	...	Kf5-e4
4	Qd7-e7 check	

Because of the Black Queen's control of the board, White actually only had two checks left, e7 and b7. From b7 he wouldn't be able to get back and give a check at b3, so he chooses e7.

4	...	Ke4-d3
5	Qe7-d7 check	Kd3-e2

Black has just about completed the first step of his plan. His King is closing in on the White King.

6	Qd7-e7 check	Qc4-e6

This move blocks any remaining checks. Notice that with the White Queen on a dark square, and the Black King on a white square, the Queen can't move along a diagonal and give a check. That's an important motif for cutting down on checks in the ending.

7	Qe7-b7	

The Queen heads for g2, to start checking again.

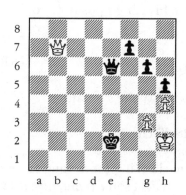

Diagram 51: Black on Move

7	...	f7-f5!

A good move, creating a square for the Queen at e4. Under some circumstances, the pawn may push on to f4, breaking up the White King's defenses.

> 8   Qb7-g2 check

White starts a new series of checks from g2.

Depending on the pawn structure, the Queen may not be especially effective checking the King from close range. The King will himself control many of the Queen's checking squares, so the Queen will always have to be located at least two squares away, and if the pawns get in the way, there may not be a lot of checking squares at that distance.

> 8   ...   Ke2-e3

Now, for instance, White has only one available check, at g1.

> 9   Qg2-b2

White moves the Queen over to the open Queenside, where there's more room for checks.

If White tries to stick close to the Kingside, he can quickly be maneuvered out of checking room. Here's a typical sequence: 9 Qg2-g1 check Ke3-e2 10 Qg1-g2 check Ke2-d3 11 Qg2-f3 check Kd2-d2 12 Qf3-f4 check Kd2-e2! and White has no more checks. The wide-open spaces on the Queenside offer White better prospects.

> 9   ...   Qe6-c4

The Black Queen gets back to the center while controlling a bunch of key checking squares.

> 10   Qb2-a3 check   Qc4-d3

Blocks the check while setting a new trap. If White plays 11 Qa3-c1 check, Black answers with Qd3-d2 check, forcing off the Queens.

11	Qa3-c5 check	Ke3-f3

This leaves White only one check, on c6.

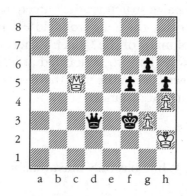

Diagram 52: White on Move

12	Qc5-c6 check	Qd3-e4

This move contains another trap, thanks to the aggressive position of Black's King. If White tries to equalize material with 13 Qc6xg6, Black forces checkmate: 13 ... Qe4-e2 check 14 Kh2-g1 Qe2-g2 checkmate.

13	Qc6-c3 check

White sees through that trap and keeps checking.

13	...	Kf3-f2

Threatening Qe4-g2 checkmate.

14	Qc3-c5 check	Qe4-e3

Black blocks the check with a new threat: 15 ... Qe3xg3 check
16 Kh2-h1 Qg3-g1 checkmate.

> 15   Qc5-c2 check

This is the only check left.

> 15   ...   Qe3-e2!

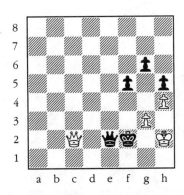

Diagram 53: White on Move

The lineup of the Black Queen and the White King on the
same rank is the beginning of the end. Now if White plays 16
Qc2-c5 check, Black has 16 ... Kf2-f3 check and 17 ... Qe2-g2
checkmate.

> 16   Qc2-c6

The best defense. White guards the g2 square, where most of
the mates occur.

> 16   ...   Kf2-f1 check!
> 17   Kh2-h3

The only square. If White plays 17 Kh2-h1, Black trades Queens
with 17 ... Qe2-e4 check!

| 17 | ... | Kf1-g1 |

Closing in. Now the threats are Qe2-h2 checkmate or Qe2-g4 checkmate or Qe2-f1 check, mating next turn.

| 18 | Qc6-c5 check | |

White has one last ingenious defensive try.

| 18 | ... | Qe2-f2 |
| 19 | Qc5-e3! | |

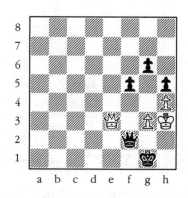

Diagram 54: Black on Move

This is it! If Black gets sloppy and grabs the Queen, 19 ... Qf2xe3, White is stalemated and the game is a draw! But Black is too sharp.

| 19 | ... | f5-f4! |

This finishes it. If 20 g3xf4, Black has 20 ... Qf2xe3 checkmate, or if 20 Qe3xf4 Qf2-g2 checkmate.

| 20 | Qe3xf2 check | Kg1xf2 |
| 21 | g3xf4 | Kf2-f3! |

Black captures the f-pawn next turn, and the h-pawn in a couple of turns. After that his own pawns Queen easily.

10. QUEEN AGAINST TWO ROOKS

One ending that occurs with some regularity is that of a lone Queen against two Rooks. Beginners favor having the Queen in this ending, since the Queen is much more powerful than either Rook separately, and coordinating the Rooks can be a tough chore. The more experienced player understands the brutal power of two Rooks in tandem, and knows that the Queen can have a difficult time holding her own.

ROOKS ON A WIDE-OPEN BOARD

Our next ending shows the power of the two Rooks against the Queen when the board is wide open and the two Rooks can cooperate against the enemy King. It's from a game in 1957 between Sammy Reshevsky (Black) and Donald Byrne (White).

Reshevsky is generally considered the second-best American player of all time, behind Bobby Fischer. He dominated American chess from the 1930s to the 1950s, when Fischer appeared on the scene, and he remained a dangerous opponent up until his retirement in the 1980s. Donald Byrne was one of the young American stars to appear in New York after World War II. His promising career was cut short by an untimely illness. His brother, Robert, still edits the chess column for the New York Times. Diagram 55 shows the position after White has played c3-c4.

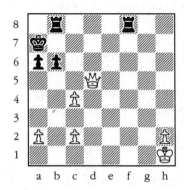

Diagram 55: Black (Reshevsky) on Move

Just counting pieces and pawns in Position 55 might leave the impression that White is doing well. He has a Queen and two pawns against Black's two Rooks. His Queen seems powerfully placed in the center of the board, while Black's Rooks do not seem very influential.

But first impressions can be deceiving. Actually, White's in serious trouble. Why? Because his pawns are all isolated.

An isolated pawn is a pawn that doesn't have a friendly pawn on either adjacent file. White's a-pawn is isolated because White doesn't have a pawn on the b-file to protect it if the need arises. The two White pawns on the c-file are isolated since there are no White pawns on the b-file or d-file. Isolated pawns can't be protected by other pawns, so they have to be protected by pieces. And that's a problem if your opponent has more pieces than you do. If Black's two Rooks both gang up to attack a White pawn, White's Queen won't be much use in the defense. The Rooks will just gobble up the pawn, then go on to attack the next one.

Actually Black has a pretty simple winning plan in Position 55. It requires these three steps:

(1) Use the Rooks in tandem to capture the White c-pawns and the h-pawn, clearing the board and exposing the White King.

(2) Herd the White King to the edge of the board.

(3) Use one Rook to keep the King trapped on the edge while the other Rook gives checkmate.

How can White fight against this plan? He only has one weapon — try to use the open board to give perpetual check with the Queen. To avoid perpetual check, the Black King will need to stay in the corner where it currently resides, and Black's Rooks will have to do double duty, guarding the approaches to the King while accomplishing the steps in Black's own plan.

Let's watch Reshevsky at work, as he shows us how to methodically make progress.

| 1 | ... | Rf8-c8 |

The first step is to clear away the White pawns. Black will start with the c-pawns, so he brings one Rook to bear on the c-file.

| 2 | Qd5-d7 check | Ka7-a8 |

Unfortunately, Black can't stick a Rook on b7 without losing the Rook on c8. So the King has to retreat.

| 3 | Kh1-g1 | |

The White King doesn't want to be on the edge of the board, so White starts to move it toward the center. The longer White can keep his King in the center, the better off he'll be.

Why doesn't White guard his attacked pawn on c4? Because he doesn't have to! The pawn is indirectly guarded. If Black tries 3 ... Rc8xc4?? White replies with 4 Qd7-d5 check! and the double attack on Black's King and Rook will win the loose Rook next turn.

Does White expect Black to fall into this trap? No. The point of noticing small traps like this is to save time.White doesn't waste a move guarding his c-pawn since it's already guarde. Instead, he just brings his King closer to the action. Seeing the threats and traps already in the position give you a way of using your pieces more efficently. That's part of what winning chess is all about.

	3	...	Rc8-c5

The Rook moves to a protected square so that the other Rook can switch over to c8, piling up on the c-pawn. Black has to maneuver slowly and carefully, so that the White Queen can't do any damage.

	4	Kg1-f1	Rb8-c8

Now that Black has doubled Rooks on the c-file, it's curtains for the front c-pawn. Even if White protects the pawn with his Queen, Black will just snap it off.

	5	h2-h4	

White will push his h-pawn as far as he can, giving Black something else to worry about.

	5	...	Rc5xc4
	6	h4-h5	

White can't do anything about the rear c-pawn either, so he doesn't bother trying. The h-pawn could cause some trouble if it advances any further.

	6	...	Rc4xc2

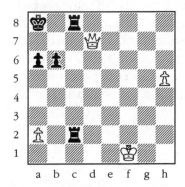

Diagram 56: White on Move

The c-pawns have fallen with no resistance. Now Black turns his attention to the pesky h-pawn.

> 7   h5-h6   Rc8-c7

A move with two purposes. The Rook on c7 guards the h7 square, preventing the White pawn from advancing further. It also forms a secure nest for Black's King. With a Rook on c7 and the King on a7, Black will be safe from any annoying checks, which will allow him to turn his full attention to the h-pawn.

> 8   Qd7-a4

Threatens Qa4xa6 check.

> 8   ...   Ka8-a7

Stops that threat. Now Black is ready to go after the h-pawn with his other Rook.

> 9   Qa4-f4   Rc2-c6

The front Rook attacks the pawn. Black now threatens Rc7-h7, ganging up on the poor pawn.

10	Kf1-e2

White can't do much about the threat, so he moves his King into the center.

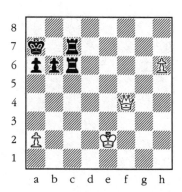

Diagram 57: Black on Move

Black could now just capture the h-pawn by playing Rc7-h7 and Rc6xh6. Instead, Black gives a series of checks, which don't really change the position, and only then captures the pawn. The reason for the series of meaningless checks is to gain time on his clock.

All tournament chess games are played with time clocks, which record the amount of time used by each player. If a player uses more than his allotted time (called overstepping the clock) he loses the game, regardless of the position on the board. A player running low on time, who sees a way to repeat a series of moves, might play those moves quickly just to improve his time situation. There's nothing unethical about such a maneuver, and if you watch a tournament you'll see that situation come up a few times.

10	...	Rc7-e7 check
11	Ke2-d3	Re7-d7 check
12	Kd3-e3	Rc6-e6 check
13	Ke3-f3	Rd7-h7

Back to the main plan.

14	Qf4-f8	Re6xh6

Diagram 58: White on Move

It would have been a mistake to capture with the other Rook. If Black had played 14 ... Rh7xh6, the seventh rank would have been left unguarded, and White would have replied with 15 Qf8-f7 check, followed by a series of checks on f8 and f7. The only way for Black to escape these checks would be to bring his King out into the open via c6, but that would open up still more checking possibilities on the wide-open board. To have a hope of winning the game, Black has to keep his King sheltered from checks, which in turn means keeping the seventh row guarded by a Rook.

Black's next step is to try to herd the White King to the edge of the board.

15	Kf3-e4	

White sees Black's plan, so he tries to keep his King in the center.

15	...	Rh6-h2

For Black's plan to work, his Rooks need to operate at a safe distance from the White King.

16	Qf8-g8	

By attacking the Rook on h7, White prevents Black from moving the other Rook off the h-file.

16	...	Rh7-d7

Black seizes control of the d-file and starts the process of herding the White King to the edge of the board. His plan is to gradually push the King toward the h-file.

17	Ke4-e3	

Black's idea was to play Rh2-e2 check, pushing the King to the f-file. White tries to prevent the plan by guarding the e2-square. Now Black has to find another way.

17	...	a6-a5
18	Qg8-e6	Rh2-h7

By lining up the Rooks on the seventh rank, Black can force his other Rook to the e-file, which will push the King towards the edge.

19	Qe6-g8	

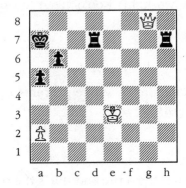

Diagram 59: Black to Move

| 19 | ... | Rh7-e7 check |

United, the Rooks can push the King to the f-file.

| 20 | Ke3-f3 | Rd7-d3 check |

This check will push the King to either f4 or f2.

| 21 | Kf3-f4 | |

White is trying to keep his King away from the edges of the board. Hence, he steers his King toward the center for as long as possible.

| 21 | ... | Rd3-d1 |

Black is aiming to play Rd1-f1 check next turn, which will push the King over to the g-file.

| 22 | Qg8-c4 | |

White guards against the threat by moving the Queen to c4, where it guards the f1 square.

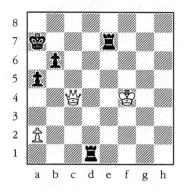

Diagram 60: Black on Move

| 22 | ... | Rd1-f1 check! |

But Black has a surprise! By noticing a tactical trick, Black's able to keep his plan on track. In this case, the tactical trick is called a skewer: If White now captures the audacious Rook with 23 Qc4xf1, Black takes advantage of the lineup of White's King and Queen on the same file and plays 23 ... Re7-f7 check! followed by 24 ... Rf7xf1. With a Rook to the good, Black would force checkmate easily.

Making progress in endings isn't just a matter of knowing grand strategical plans. You'll also need an alert eye for tactics like this, to push your plan forward at critical moments. (For more examples of the skewer and other tactics, see the book Winning Chess Tactics in the Road to Chess Mastery series.)

| 23 | Kf4-g5 |

The White King is being forced even closer to the edge of the board.

| 23 | ... | Re7-g7 check! |

This pushes the King right to the edge, the h-file.

24   Kg5-h6

A good move, reaching the edge but attacking the Black Rook at the same time. If White had instead moved 24 Kg5-h4?, Black could have checkmated at once with Rf1-h1. Now if Black checks on h1, White's King just captures the Rook on g7.

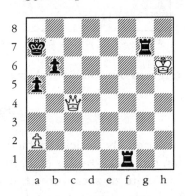

Diagram 61: Black on Move

24   ...   Rf1-g1

Both Black Rooks were under attack, so he pauses for a second to consolidate his gains. With the King on the edge of the board, Black needs to regroup his Rooks for a mating attack.

25   Qc4-d4

White centers his Queen and attacks the Black Rook on g7.

There's no real threat here. Notice that even if White captures on g7 (26 Qd4xg7 Rg1xg7 27 Kh6xg7), White's King is too far away to stop the Black pawns. Black would just play b6-b5! and eventually Queen one of his pawns. That's why it was so important for Black to pick up all the White pawns at the beginning of the ending. Any endgames that might result from trading off the major pieces are now lost for White.

| 25 | ... | Rg1-g4 |

Hoping White will fall into the trap of exchanging pieces.

| 26 | Qd4-d8 | |

White sees the trap and just tries to keep his Queen active.

26	...	Rg4-g6 check
27	Kh6-h5	Rg6-g2
28	Kh5-h6	

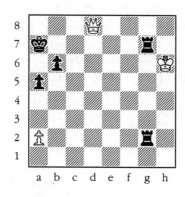

Diagram 62: Black on Move

Black's plan has stalled a bit. Although White's King is on the edge of the board, it's the wrong edge. As long as Black's Rook on g7 is tied to the seventh rank (to prevent White from starting an infinite series of checks on the Black King), Black can't make any more progress. White will keep attacking the Rook with his King, and Black's other Rook will be tied down to protecting the one on g7.

The solution is to somehow chase the White King to the eighth rank (the top edge of the board). Then Black's Rooks on the seventh rank will simultaneously protect the Black King while launching checkmating threats against the White King. How is that to be accomplished? Let's watch Reshevsky pull it off.

| 28 | ... | Rg7-b7! |

The Rook gets away from the White King, but still keeps a grip on the seventh rank to prevent checks to the Black King.

| 29 | Qd8-d5 |

Attacking the Rook on g2.

| 29 | ... | Rg2-c2! |

Black's idea is to operate against the White King using the ranks (horizontal rows), rather than the files (vertical rows). Black is also taking advantage of the fact that his pawn on b6 controls the c5 square. Now if White tries to get his King back to the center by 30 Kh6-g5?, Black will play 30 ... Rc2-c5!, pinning the White Queen to the King. (Those tactical ideas again!)

| 30 | Qd5-b3 |

The Queen gets out of the Rook's way.

| 30 | ... | Rc2-c5! |

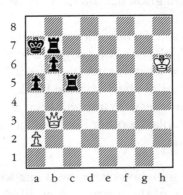

Diagram 63: White on Move

Take a look. By repositioning his Rooks, Black has sandwiched the White King to the sixth rank. The next job is to push it to the seventh.

31   Qb3-e3

The best White can do is to keep his Queen centered, trying to counter Black's maneuvers as they develop.

31   ...   Rb7-d7

Now Black threatens 32 ... Rd7-d6 check followed by Rc5-c7 check, pushing the King to the eighth row. White has to counter this plan or he's cooked.

32   Qe3-e6!

The Queen guards the d6 square, temporarily stopping Black's plan.

32   ...   Rd7-c7

Black switches to a new idea: Rc7-c6, pinning the White Queen to the King and winning the Queen for a Rook. White must move the Queen to safety.

33   Qe6-e4

The Queen steps away but remains centralized.

34   ...   Rc7-c6 check
35   Kh6-g7

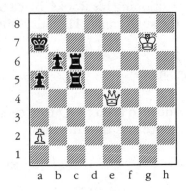

Diagram 64: Black on Move

Black has made some progress. The White King is now on the
seventh rank, just one row away from the target, the eighth rank.
But how does Black consolidate his gains? He'd like to leave his
Rook on c6, keeping the White King where it is, and maneuver
the other Rook to give check somewhere on the seventh rank.
That would push White to the eighth. Unfortunately, the Rook
on c5 needs to stay where it is to guard the Rook on c6. And if
the Rook on c6 moves back to c7, then the White King skips
back to the sixth rank. How can Black untangle his Rooks to
make further progress?

35	...	Ka7-b7!

The Black King has to do its part. By guarding the Rook on c6,
he frees the other Rook for offensive maneuvers. And notice
that with White's King now on the seventh rank, Black doesn't
have to worry about checks anymore. If White tries 36 Qe4-e7
check??, Black replies 36 ... Rc6-c7, pinning the Queen to her
own King!

36	Kg7-f7	Rc5-h5!

The freed Rook jumps into action with a threat: Rh5-h7 check!

37	Kf7-g7

Stops that threat for the moment.

> 37   ...   Rh5-h6!

Black has a new threat: 38 ... Rh6-d6 followed by 39 ... Rd6-d7 check.

As before, White has the opportunity to win both opposing Rooks for his own Queen. He could play 38 Qe4-e7 check Rc6-c7 39 Qe7xc7 check Kb7xc7 40 Kg7xh6. However, his King would still be too far away from Black's pawns, and Black would play b6-b5! followed by eventually Queening a pawn.

> 38   Kg7-f8

White couldn't stop the threat, but by leaving his Queen on e4, he prevents either of the Black Rooks from moving to the seventh rank. The Queen guards h7, while it pins the other Rook.

> 38   ...   Rh6-h8 check!

This check does the trick for Black. By forcing the King back to the seventh rank, Black sets up another tactical trick.

> 39   Kf8-e7

Diagram 65: Black on Move

39	...	Rh8-h7 check!

Here's the idea. If White captures the Rook by Qe4xh7, Black has another skewer: Rc6-c7 check followed by Rc7xh7. Once again, Black makes progress by seeing more deeply into the tactics of the position.

40	Ke7-d8	

Now White is trapped on the eighth rank — permanently. Black's job now is to work out a checkmating maneuver. First he has to coordinate his Rooks again.

41	...	Rh7-c7

This guards the c6 Rook, which enables the King to move, thus unpinning the Rook and letting the Rook move. Once Black unties the knot, both Rooks will be active, and White will be finished.

42	Qe4-d5	Kb7-a7

Now the Rook at c6 is free to move.

43	Qd5-e5	Rc7-b7!

The Rook slips away from the White King's attack allowing the other Rook to move to the seventh rank.

44	Qe5-g5	Rc6-b7!

With two Rooks lined up on the seventh rank, Black can generate multiple checkmating threats.

45	Qg5-e5	

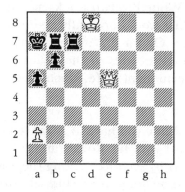

Diagram 66: Black on Move

| 46 | ... | Rc7-h7 |

The end of a long road. Black's first threat is just 47 ... Rb7-b8 check, which forces White to give up his Queen to stop mate.

If White prevents this threat by playing 47 Kd7-c7, Black just plays 47 ... Rh7-h8 check! 48 Qe5xh8 Rb7-b8 check, followed by 49 ... Rb8xh8. Either way, Black ends up a Rook ahead, so White finally gives up.

USING THE KING

In the next ending, White's problem is a little more difficult.

Diagram 67: Black on Move

On the plus side, White has two Rooks against a Queen, plus an extra pawn. That would normally be enough of an advantage for an easy win. On the downside, he has only two remaining pawns, on opposite sides of the board. That means his King lacks any permanent, safe haven from Black's Queen checks.

To win the game, White will have to advance his King into the middle of the board with his Rooks, and use it as a fighting piece to help his pawns advance. Along the way, he'll pick off Black's h-pawn at some point to give himself two passed pawns. It's a plan which requires ingenuity and patience, but it can be done, and we'll show you how.

This ending arose from a recent game between Anatoly Karpov and Viswanathan Anand. Karpov took over the World Championship when Bobby Fischer retired in 1975, and held it for ten years, until he was defeated by Garry Kasparov. He remains today one of the world's top five players. His play is careful and accurate; at his best, he exploits small positional advantages with great precision, slowly squeezing his opponents until their positions collapse. Anand is the finest player ever to emerge from India, and he is also currently rated one of the world's top-five. In 1995, he lost a close match for the World Championship to Kasparov.

1	...	Qa2-c2

Black's Queen is a little offside in the position (he just captured a White pawn on a2) so Black prepares to centralize it.

2	Rf1-f2!

The two Rooks now provide cover for the White King to enter the game via g2 and g3. Remember, the King will have to be a fighting piece in this ending, since it has no hiding places in the corners of the board.

It might seem incredible that a King can venture out into the middle of an open board when the opponent has a Queen and plenty of room to maneuver. But as we'll see, two Rooks can guard a lot of squares.

> 2   ...   Qc2-e4

Checks don't necessarily do any good. After 2 ... Qc2-d1 check 3 Kh1-g2, Black is already out of checks. If Black tries 2 ... Qc2-b1 check 3 Kh1-g2 Qb1-g6 check??, White wins immediately with 4 Rf3-g3!, pinning the Queen.

Instead, Black just pins the front Rook. His strategy is just to be as much of a nuisance as possible, putting obstacles in White's path and hoping for a blunder.

> 3   Kh1-g2

The King begins marching to the center.

> 3   ...   Qe4-b4

The Queen blocks the b-pawn while preventing the White King from crossing the fourth rank.

> 4   Rf2-e2

One point of this move is to opens a path for the White King to advance, via f2. The more important point is to reposition this Rook in front of the Rook on f3, controlling more space. (The f3 Rook can't move for now without losing the b-pawn.)

> 4   ...   Qb4-d4

Guards the f2-square, preventing the White King from marching that way.

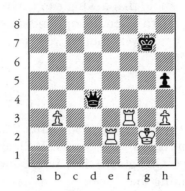

Diagram 68: White on Move

5	Re2-e7 check	Kg7-g6
6	Re7-e6 check	Kg6-g7
7	Rf3-g3 check	Kg7-f7
8	Rg3-e3!	

This was White's idea all along — to reposition his Rooks so that one Rook controls the sixth rank while the other, from e3, guards both pawns. Now the White King can advance into the center of the board.

8	...	Qd4-d5 check

Black will still try to disrupt White's plans by giving check whenever possible. Unfortunately, the White Rooks control most of the key squares on the board.

9	Kg2-g3	

The King heads toward the center. Depending on how Black plays, White's King can take one of several routes: Kg3-f4-e5 or Kg3-h4xh5, or Kg3-f2-e2-d3. Black can block some of these routes but not all of them.

9	...	Qd5-g5 check

Black decides to control the f4 and h4 squares, saving his h-pawn at the same time. White has to head back toward f2.

10   Kg3-f2

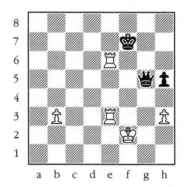

Diagram 69: Black on Move

10   ...   Qg5-h4 check

Not the best square for the Queen (on the side of the board and blocked in by pawns) but it's the only check available. Notice that if Black plays 10 ... Qg5-f5 check or Qg5-f4 check, White replies with 11 Re3-f3!, pinning the Black Queen against the Black King. That doesn't win the Queen outright, since Black would play 11 ... Qxf3 check 12 Kf2xf3 Kf7xe6, trading the Queen for two Rooks. Unfortunately for Black, though, the King and pawn ending would be hopelessly lost. White would advance his b-pawn as a decoy, driving the Black King over to the b-file, then capture Black's h-pawn with his King, eventually Queening his own h-pawn.

One of White's hidden strengths in this endgame is that all King and pawn endings are won for him in just that way, so Black has to be very careful about aligning his King and Queen on the same rank or file. That's another way in which Black's checking possibilities are severely limited.

11   Kf2-e2

The King heads for d3 and points north and west.

11   ...   Qh4-d4

The Queen had totally run out of checks, so she blocks the King from moving to the d-file.

12   Re6-e4!

White can't be too rigid about where he places his Rooks. The ideal formation may well be on e3 and e6, but he will still have to maneuver to force his King forward.

12   ...   Qd4-a1

Black has to decide whether he wants to allow the White King to penetrate the Queenside or the Kingside. If Black checks on b2, the White King moves to f3 and then f4, threatening the pawn on h5. Black decides to prevent this maneuvering by going to a1, preparing to move to f1 if necessary. However, this allows the White King into d3 and then c4. Black can only prevent one line of attack: He decides that saving his h-pawn is top priority for now.

13   Ke2-d3   Kf7-f6

Checks don't help, as they just drive the White King where he wants to go. The Queen is well-placed right now, keeping the White King out of c3 and d4, so Black improves the position of his King.

14   Re4-e6 check

White resumes the preferred placing of his Rooks, on e6 and e3, where they guard many of the critical squares the Queen will need to access to give perpetual check.

14	...	Kf6-f5

There's no future for the King at f7. From f5 he's ready to guard the h-pawn.

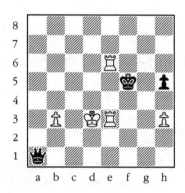

Diagram 70: White on Move

15	b3-b4!	

White starts the next phase of his plan. Now that his King is centered, he's going to move the pawn from b3 to b6 where it will be guarded by the front Rook. On the intermediate squares, b4 and b5, the King will take over the job of guarding the pawn.

15	...	Qa1-c1

Cuts the White King off from the b-file. Checks don't help, as any check just forces the King to c4, where he wants to go anyway.

16	Kd3-d4	

Now White is ready to push the pawn on to b5 next turn.

16	...	Qc1-c8

Still keeping the King off the c-file.

      17   b4-b5!

Now the pawn can't be stopped from reaching b6.

      17   ...   Qc8-d8 check

Since he can't stop the pawn, Black decides to give a few checks.

      18   Kd4-c5   Qd8-c7 check
      19   Kc5-b4   Qc7-f4 check
      20   Kb4-b3!

As we learned in the last chapter, the best way to avoid checks is to keep the King on a square of the opposite color from the one the enemy Queen is on. This eliminates checks along most of the diagonals.

Now Black is out of checks again. Take a look at the next diagram, in which the squares controlled by the White pieces and pawns are marked with an 'x':

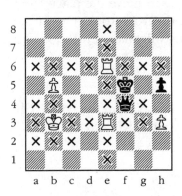

Diagram 71: 'x' Marks the Squares that White Controls

The diagram makes Black's problem clear. The only areas of the board where the Queen can freely move to give check are off in the corners. White controls almost the whole center section with his pieces. Instead of a powerful piece controlling the flow of events, Black's Queen is more like a hunted fugitive, taking pot shots from long-range.

20	...	Qf4-c7

There's no future over on the King-side, so Black repositions the Queen to at least prevent the pawn from moving to b7.

21	b5-b6!	

Mission accomplished. The pawn sits well-protected, just two squares from Queening.

21	...	Qc7-d7

Again, from a Black square the Queen has no checks, so Black repositions the Queen to a White square. Now some checking possibilities open up (b5, d5, and d1).

22	Re3-e5 check	

With the pawn now safe at b6, White decides to check for awhile with his Rooks, to see where Black will place his King.

22	...	Kf5-f4

A forced play.

23	Re5-e4 check	Kf4-g3

Not a good idea. Black had nothing better than Kf4-f5, repeating the position. Black's move looks aggressive, but now his King gets cut off from his own h-pawn.

24	Re4-e3 check	Kg3-h2

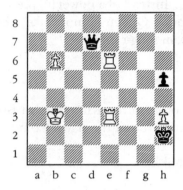

Diagram 72: White on Move

Black's King is stuck in the corner, trapped by White's Rook at
e3. White now embarks on a new plan. With the Black King
cut off, White's own King heads toward the Black pawn.

      25   Kb3-c4!

The pawn will prove very hard to defend with a White King in
the vicinity.

      25   ...   h5-h4

No need to move the Queen, which right now is preventing the
King from crossing the d-file. Meanwhile, the pawn is just as
safe here as on h5.

      26   Kc4-c5

To get to the King-side, White will have to operate with double
threats. Now White is threatening Re6-e7, followed by the advance of the b-pawn.

      26   ...   Qd7-c8 check

Chases the King away from the c5-c6 area. The b-pawn is White's most dangerous threat, so the Black Queen has to keep an eye on it.

> 27   Kc5-d5!

A move like 27 Re6-c6, blocking the check, might look tempting, but Black would reply with 27 ... Qc8-f5 check, and with his Rooks disconnected, White would have to be very careful. After 28 Kc5-d6, for instance, Black would have a double attack with 28 ... Qf5-f4 check!, and after 29 Re3-e5 (the only move to save the Rook), Black would gobble a pawn with 29 ... Kh2xh3.

Keeping the Rooks connected until the right moment is the surest way to win.

> 27   ...   Qc8-d8 check
> 28   Kd5-e4!

The King heads for h4 and the Black pawn. Again, staying on a square of the opposite color from the Black Queen's square minimizes the checks.

> 28   ...   Qd8-d7

Stops the b-pawn from moving.

> 29   Ke4-f5

Continues on track toward the h-pawn.

> 29   ...   Kh2-g2

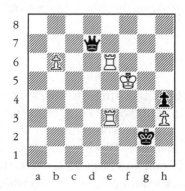

Diagram 73: White on Move

> 30   Kf5-g5

Finally White attacks the h-pawn.

> 30   ...   Qd7-g7 check

Black could defend the pawn with 30 ... Qd7-h7, but the Queen would be left out of play. White would reply with 31 Kg5-g4! and suddenly Black would be facing mating threats. White would be ready to play 32 Re3-e2 check Kg2-f1 33 Re2-e1 check Kf1-f2 34 Re6-e2 checkmate. Black could move his Queen and prevent the checkmate, but he'd have to give up the pawn anyway.

> 31   Kg5xh4   Kg2-f2

Hoping to play to f3 if White checks on e2.

> 32   Re3-e5

There's no need to keep the Rook on the third rank any longer. With the Black pawn eliminated, White doesn't have to worry about protecting his own h-pawn. (White's b-pawn is enough to win the game.) The next job is to get the King back toward the Queenside.

| 32 | ... | Qg7-h8 check |

Black tries to keep the King busy with checks.

| 33 | Kh4-g4 | Qh8-g7 check |
| 34 | Kg4-f5 | Qg7-h7 check |

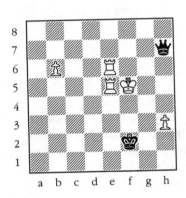

Diagram 74: White on Move

| 35 | Kf5-f6! |

White sees that he doesn't need to guard the h-pawn, because it's indirectly protected by tactics. If Black now plays 35 ... Qh7xh3, the sequence is 36 Re5-e2 check Kf2-f1 37 Re2-e1 check Kf1-f2 38 Re6-e2 check Kf2-g3 39 Re2-e3 check! winning the Queen with a skewer. So White just keeps pushing his King forward. Noticing these tactical tricks can make the difference between winning a tough game or settling for a draw.

| 35 | ... | Qh7-h4 check |

Black sees White's trap, and continues his checks.

| 36 | Kf6-f7 |

Heading for e8 and the Queenside. But another new possibility has opened up, which White might be able to exploit instead. His Rooks can now operate against the Black King on the files. For instance, if it were White's move now, he could play 37 Re5-f5 check Kf2-g2 38 Re6-g6 check Kg2-h2. This sequence wouldn't lead to checkmate (yet) but it would force the Black King in the corner, and it's definitely an idea to keep in mind for the future.

Always be prepared to revise your original game plan when new ideas open up.

| 36 | ... | Qh4-h7 check |
| 37 | Kf7-e8 | Qh7-b7 |

If Black grabs the h-pawn, White wins with the maneuver Re5-e2 check, Re2-e1 check, and Re6-e2 check, as we noticed before. But there's now another reason for leaving the h-pawn on the board: It provides Black's King with some much-needed cover from the rampaging White Rooks.

| 38 | h3-h4! |

On the other hand, by not taking the pawn, Black leaves White the option to just march this pawn up the board as well. Since it doesn't disturb the position, White might as well march this pawn as far as it goes.

38	...	Qb7-b8 check
39	Ke8-f7	Qb8-b7 check
40	Kf7-g6	

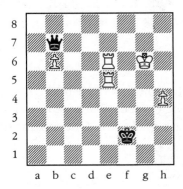

Diagram 75: Black on Move

White controls so much of the board that Black runs out of checks very quickly. If Black now plays his last check, 40 ... Qb7-g2 check, White has 41 Kg6-f6! and there are no more checks. (41 ... Qg2-f3 check is answered by 42 Re5-f5! pinning the Black Queen.)

40	...	Qb7-b8

Black aims for Qb8-g8 check, which keeps the Queen in play and continues to guard against the advance of the b-pawn.

41	h4-h5

The advance of the h-pawn opens a second front. The pawns are now equally threatening.

41	...	Qb8-g8 check

Keeping White busy is all Black can do.

42	Kg6-f5	Qg8-h7 check

This is the right checking square. If Black checks on f8, White blocks with 43 Re6-f6! and then when White's King next moves, it will be with a discovered check. For example, 42 ... Qg8-f8

check   43 Re6-f6   Qf8-c8 check   44 Kf5-g6 discovered check
Kf2-g2 45 Re5-g5 check, and Black's King is in serious trouble.

43 ·   Kf5-f6!

Black's only checks now are from h8 or h6, and those aren't
ideal squares for the Queen. Black wants to keep the Queen as
centralized as possible, else the Queen runs out of checks too
quickly.

43   ...   Kf2-f3!

Sometimes the best defense lies in doing nothing. Right now
neither White pawn can advance and the King can't move forward either, so Black just bides time with his King.

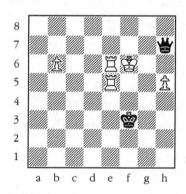

Diagram 76: White on Move

44   Re5-e3 check

White's a little stuck in his current formation, so he starts to
rearrange his Rooks.

44   ...   Kf3-f2
45   Kf6-g5   Qh7-g8 check
46   Kg5-h4   Qg8-d8 check

Black's only check.

      47   Kh4-h3

By moving toward the Black King, White has eliminated many of Black's checks while opening up some checkmating possibilities.

      47   ...   Qd8-d1?

Black is trying to get to h1 for a check, but he overlooks a maneuver by White that finishes the game off immediately.

      48   Re3-e2 check!

If Black now moves to f1, White plays Re2-e1 check! and trades his two Rooks for Black's Queen. After that he can Queen either or both of his pawns. So Black's replay is forced.

      48   ...   Kf2-f3
      49   Re2-e1!

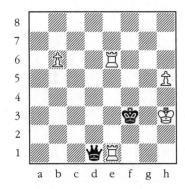

Diagram 77: Black Resigns

With the Rooks both separated from the Black King, White has two deadly threats, Re6-f6 check or Re1-f1 check, which will either be checkmate or will win Black's Queen for a Rook. Black gives up. A great ending by Karpov!

DRAWING WITH THE QUEEN

The two Rooks don't always beat a Queen. Sometimes the Queen can hold its own or even win. In order to survive or even triumph, the Queen needs to be able to prevent cooperation between the two Rooks. Here are some of the factors that help the Queen:

More pawns. This is a curious asset, since, as we have learned, the usual rule in endings is that the weaker side tries to trade pawns and get down to an ending with no pawns on the board at all. That strategy doesn't work well in a situation where the Queen faces two Rooks, since as the pawns go off the board, the Rooks wreak havoc on the wide-open lines. The presence of a lot of pawns can jam up the Rook's activity.

Weak pawns. A single weak pawn might require tying up a whole Rook to defend it, effectively cutting the Rooks' power in half.

Weak King position. If the side with the Rooks has an exposed King, the Queen may be able to set up perpetual check threats.

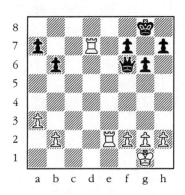

Diagram 78: Black on Move

In Diagram 78, White seems to be doing well. The pawns are even, and his two Rooks control the two center files. White is even threatening Rd7xa7 or Re2-e7, both of which look like winning moves. However, Black can take advantage of the factors mentioned above to generate just enough counterplay to save the game. Let's watch and see how he does it.

| 1 | ... | Qf6-c6! |

A good move with a double threat: Qc6xd7 and Qc6-c1 check followed by mate. White has to defend against the checkmate; he doesn't have time to rip off the pawn on a7.

| 2 | Rd7-d1 | |

Meets the threat, at the cost of being pushed on the defensive, at least temporarily.

| 2 | ... | g6-g5! |

Good chess is about anticipation. The best formation of pawns for guarding the White King is pawns on f2-g3-h4, with the King tucked away on h2. From that position, and as long as the pawn on f2 is defended somehow by a Rook, no checks are possible, and the pawns all guard each other. Black understands this, so he takes immediate measures to make sure that White will have to settle for a weaker, less desireable formation by preventing the White pawn from reaching h4.

| 3 | h2-h3 | |

White has to create some air space for his King so that the Rook on d1 is free to roam.

| 3 | ... | Kg8-g7 |

The King avoids any checks and gets closer to the action.

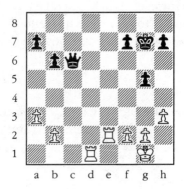

Diagram 79: White on Move

| 4 | b2-b4 |

White grabs more space on the Queenside, but now the a3-pawn could come under attack. The pawns on b2 and f2 only required one Rook to defend them both. Pawns on a3 and f2 could be tougher to defend.

| 4 | ... | Kg7-g6 |

The King gets ready to play an active role in opening up the Kingside. Black needs to open lines to the White King to set up a possible perpetual check.

| 5 | g2-g3 |

White has now created a safe spot at h2 for his King.

| 5 | ... | h7-h5! |

No sooner has White created a haven than Black tries to blast it open. Now he's ready to proceed with h5-h4 or g5-g4, as the occasion warrants.

| 6 | Re2-e7 |

White decides that his King's position is as safe as it can be, so he sends a Rook after the a7-pawn.

6   ...   f7-f6!

Black doesn't have enough pieces to tie them down to passive defense. Instead he shelters his King from checks along the sixth rank, and prepares a counter-attack if White sends his Rook off to a7.

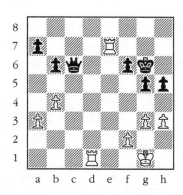

Diagram 80: White on Move

Now White sees that his Kingside could come under a strong attack if he captures the a-pawn with his Rook. Here's a possible sequence. After 7 Re7xa7, Black would play 7 ... Qc6-f3! attacking the Rook on d1 and the pawn on a3. Then after 8 Rd1-e1, h5-h4! starts to open up the Kingside. After 9 Re1-e3 Qf3-d1 check 10 Kg1-h2 Qd1-f1, White appears to be able to guard everything with 11 Re3-f3. But Black can play 11 ... g5-g4!!, and after 12 h3xg4 h4-h3!!, White actually gets checkmated. This variation isn't forced, and White has other defensive tries, but it shows how dangerous the Queen can be when the Rooks are disconnected and only one remains to defend against a rampaging Queen.

7   Re7-e3

White sees that he can get into trouble if he goes too far afield, so he drops back to try something else.

| 7 | ... | Kg6-g7 |

Black doesn't see a good way to improve his position at this point, so he plays a waiting move to see if White has a real plan.

| 8 | g3-g4? | |

White comes up with a bad idea. This creates a pawn which is both weak and easily attacked — a bad combination. Now Black can get a solid draw by tying White's pieces down to defending this pawn.

| 8 | ... | h5xg4 |
| 9 | h3xg4 | Qc6-c4! |

Black immediately moves to attack the pawn.

| 10 | Re3-g3 | |

The White Rook guards both the pawn on g4 and the pawn on a3, but with one Rook tied down, he doesn't have enough ammunition to make progress in other parts of the board.

10	...	Kg7-g6
11	Rd1-d3	Qc4-c1 check
12	Kg1-h2	Qc1-f4

Black doesn't have to do anything concrete to get his draw — it's enough just to make small threats and prevent White from doing anything.

13	Rd3-f3	Qf4-d6
14	Rf3-f5	a7-a6
15	Kh2-h1	Qd6-d1 check
16	Kh1-h2	

Here the game was given up as a draw. White can't make any progress as long as one of his Rooks was tied to the defense of the g4-pawn.

Moral: The Rooks don't look powerful when they're tied down defending weak pawns. To assert their superiority, the Rooks need a wide-open board to roam.

TACTICAL TRICKS

Not every ending requires long, drawn-out strategy to win. Sometimes you just have to be alert to tactical strokes that lie just below the surface of the position. Here are two amazing examples of what's possible when you stay alert, even if your opponent has a mighty Queen.

Diagram 81: White on Move

White looks to be in some trouble in Diagram 81. Black has just played his Queen to f2, attacking the White Rook. Obviously White can't capture the Queen, since then Black would play g3xf2, and the pawn would Queen next turn. But if White moves his Rook away, say with Rf1-b1, Black plays f5-f4!, and he's threatening to push on to f3 next turn, with checkmating threats.

What's White to do?

Answer — stay alert, and look at all the legal checks and captures! When former World Champion Alexander Alekhine encountered this, he found his way clear to an easy win with some tactical alertness. Here's how he played:

>   1   Rf1xf2!!

Incredible. How will White be able to stop the pawn on f2 from Queening?

>   1   ...   g3xf2

Now what?

>   2   Rd5xf5!!

Well, this certainly stops the pawn for one turn anyway. But there's a subtle point.

>   2   ...   Kg6xf5
>   3   g2-g4 check!

The final twist. White moves the g2-pawn with a tempo check, clearing the way for his King to get to g2.

>   3   ...   Kf5xg4
>   4   Kh1-g2

The White King stops the pawn. Now his own pawn at a5 will Queen before Black can get his h-pawn moving. Brilliant!

Alekhine strikes again in this next neat endgame maneuver:

Diagram 82: Black on Move

This time the White Queen faces a combination of a Black Rook and a Black Knight. Black also has a strong passed pawn, ready to Queen. But White has the Queening square under guard, and if Black moves the Rook off the second rank, White will play Kg3xh2.

Meanwhile, the Black Knight is pinned by the White Queen. (A good thing, since otherwise Black would win by Nf6-e4 check.) Unpinning the Knight looks difficult, though, since if Black retreats his King, White will start checking with his Queen on c7 or b7. If Black evades the checks by going back to the sixth rank, White will just move his Queen back to c6 with another pin. Does Alekhine have a winning idea?

He does, and it's quite a nice one.

| 1 | ... | Kg6-h5! |

Black abandons the pinned Knight and walks into a checkmating net. Method, or madness?

| 2 | Qc6xf6 | |

Now what? If Black Queens his pawn, White plays Qf6-g5 checkmate.

2   ...   h2-h1 (N) checkmate!

Diagram 83: White is Checkmated

Black underpromotes to a Knight, and White gets checkmated first.

Stay alert — it pays!

11. NEXT STEPS

You've now completed this introduction to endgame play involving Queens and Rooks. If you're like most players, it's been full of surprises for you. You've seen the power of a passed pawn, the importance of precise calculation, and the strength of a fighting King, even on an open board against a Queen.

As you saw in this book, many endings hinge on a ability to spot tactical chances. Be sure to read "Winning Chess Tactics" in the Road to Chess Mastery series. You'll learn how to spot all the basic tactical ideas, including skewers, pins, and double attacks. Also, be sure to read the companion book, "Basic Endgame Strategy: Kings, Pawns, and Minor Pieces," for more winning endgame ideas.

As you practice, don't be content with just reading or playing against your local circle of friends. Try to locate clubs or tournaments in your area where you can meet new people and play in organized competitions. You'll meet a lot of folks who share your interests, and you'll improve much faster. The book "Beginning Chess Play" has some tips for tracking down the clubs in your area.

Most of all, keep reading, keep playing, and keep winning!

CARDOZA PUBLISHING CHESS BOOKS

- OPENINGS -

WINNING CHESS OPENINGS *by Bill Robertie* - Shows concepts and best opening moves of more than 25 essential openings from Black's and White's perspectives: King's Gambit, Center Game, Scotch Game, Giucco Piano, Vienna Game, Bishop's Opening, Ruy Lopez, French, Caro-Kann, Sicilian, Alekhine, Pirc, Modern, Queen's Gambit, Nimzo-Indian, Queen's Indian, Dutch, King's Indian, Benoni, English, Bird's, Reti's, and King's Indian Attack. Examples from 25 grandmasters and champions including Fischer and Kasparov. 144 pages, $9.95

WORLD CHAMPION OPENINGS *by Eric Schiller* - This serious reference work covers the essential opening theory and moves of every major chess opening and variation as played by *all* the world champions. Reading as much like an encyclopedia of the must-know openings crucial to every chess player's knowledge as a powerful tool showing the insights, concepts and secrets as used by the greatest players of all time, *World Champion Openings (WCO)* covers an astounding 100 crucial openings in full conceptual detail (with 100 actual games from the champions themselves)! *A must-have book for serious chess players.* 384 pages, $18.95

STANDARD CHESS OPENINGS *by Eric Schiller* - The new definitive standard on opening chess play in the 20th century, this comprehensive guide covers every important chess opening and variation ever played and currently in vogue. In all, more than 3,000 opening strategies are presented! Differing from previous opening books which rely almost exclusively on bare notation, *SCO* features substantial discussion and analysis on each opening so that you learn and understand the concepts behind them. Includes more than 250 completely annotated games (including a game representative of each major opening) and more than 1,000 diagrams! For modern players at any level, this is the standard reference book necessary for competitive play. *A must have for serious chess players!!!* 768 pages, $24.95

UNORTHODOX CHESS OPENINGS *by Eric Schiller* - The exciting guide to all the major unorthodox openings used by chess players, contains more than 1,500 weird, contentious, controversial, unconventional, arrogant, and outright strange opening strategies. From their tricky tactical surprises to their bizarre names, these openings fly in the face of tradition. You'll meet such openings as the Orangutang, Raptor Variation, Halloween Gambit, Double Duck, Frankenstein-Dracula Variation, and even the Drunken King! These openings are a sexy and exotic way to spice up a game and a great weapon to spring on unsuspecting and often unprepared opponents. More than 750 diagrams show essential positions. 528 pages, $24.95

GAMBIT OPENING REPERTOIRE FOR WHITE *by Eric Schiller* - Chessplayers who enjoy attacking from the very first move are rewarded here with a powerful repertoire of brilliant gambits. Starting off with 1.e4 or 1.d4 and then using such sharp weapons such as the Göring Gambit (Accepted and Declined), Halasz Gambit, Alapin Gambit, Ulysses Gambit, Short Attack and many more, to put great pressure on opponents, Schiller presents a complete attacking repertoire to use against the most popular defenses, including the Sicilian, French, Scandinavian, Caro-Kann, Pirc, Alekhine, and other Open Game positions. 192 pages, $14.95.

GAMBIT OPENING REPERTOIRE FOR BLACK *by Eric Schiller* - For players that like exciting no-holds-barred chess, this versatile gambit repertoire shows Black how to take charge with aggressive attacking defenses against any orthodox first White opening move; 1.e4, 1.d4 and 1.c4. Learn the Scandinavian Gambit against 1.e4, the Schara Gambit and Queen's Gambit Declined variations against 1.d4, and some flank and unorthodox gambits also. Black learns the secrets of seizing the initiative from White's hands, usually by investing a pawn or two, to begin powerful attacks that can send White to early defeat. 176 pages, $14.95.

COMPLETE DEFENSE TO QUEEN PAWN OPENINGS *by Eric Schiller* - This aggressive counterattacking repertoire covers Black opening systems against virtually every chess opening except for 1.e4 (including most flank games), based on the exciting and powerful Tarrasch Defense, an opening that helped bring Championship titles to Kasparov and Spassky. Black learns to effectively use the Classical Tarrasch, Symmetrical Tarrasch, Asymmetrical Tarrasch, Marshall and Tarrasch Gambits, and Tarrasch without Nc3, to achieve an early equality or even an outright advantage in the first few moves. 288 pages, $16.95.

COMPLETE DEFENSE TO KING PAWN OPENINGS *by Eric Schiller* - Learn a complete defensive system against 1.e4. This powerful repertoire not only limits White's ability to obtain any significant opening advantage but allows Black to adopt the flexible Caro-Kann formation, the favorite weapon of many of the greatest chess players. All White's options are explained in detail, and a plan is given for Black to combat them all. Analysis is up-to-date and backed by examples drawn from games of top stars. Detailed index lets you follow the opening from the point of a specific player, or through its history. 240 pages, $16.95.

SECRETS OF THE SICILIAN DRAGON *by GM Eduard Gufeld and Eric Schiller* - The mighty Dragon Variation of the Sicilian Defense is one of the most exciting openings in chess. Everything from opening piece formation to the endgame, including clear explanations of all the key strategic and tactical ideas, is covered in full conceptual detail. Instead of memorizing a jungle of variations, you learn the really important ideas behind the opening, and how to adapt them at the chessboard. Special sections on the heroes of the Dragon show how the greatest players handle the opening. The most instructive book on the Dragon written! 208 pages, $14.95.

- MIDDLEGAME/TACTICS/WINNING CONCEPTS -

10 MOST COMMON CHESS MISTAKES and How to Fix Them *by Larry Evans* - This fascinating collection of 218 errors, oversights, and outright blunders, will not only show you the price that great players pay for violating basic principles, but how you can avoid these mistakes in your own game. You'll be challenged to choose between two moves; the right one, or the one actually played in the game. From neglecting development, king safety, misjudging threats, and premature attacks, to impulsiveness, snatching pawns, and basic inattention, you will get a complete course in exactly where you can go wrong and how to fix it. 256 pages, $14.95.

WORLD CHAMPION COMBINATIONS *by Keene and Schiller* - Learn the insights, concepts and moves of the greatest combinations ever by the greatest players who ever lived. From Morphy to Alekhine, to Fischer to Kasparov, the incredible combinations and brilliant sacrifices of the 13 World Champions are collected here in the most insightful combinations book written. Packed with fascinating strategems, 50 annotated games, and great practical advice for your own games, this is a great companion guide to *World Champion Openings*. 264 pages, $16.95.

WINNING CHESS TACTICS *by Bill Robertie* - 14 chapters of winning tactical concepts show the complete explanations and thinking behind every tactical concept: pins, single and double forks, double attacks, skewers, discovered and double checks, multiple threats - and other crushing tactics to gain an immediate edge over opponents. Learn the power tools of tactical play to become a stronger player. Includes guide to chess notation. 128 pages, $9.95

ENCYCLOPEDIA OF CHESS WISDOM, The Essential Concepts and Strategies of Smart Chess Play *by Eric Schiller* - The most important concepts, strategies, tactics, wisdom, and thinking that every chessplayer must know, plus the gold nuggets of knowledge behind every attack and defense, is collected together in one highly focused volume. From opening, middle and endgame strategy, to psychological warfare and tournament tactics, the *Encyclopedia of Chess Wisdom* forms the blueprint of power play and advantage at the chess board. Step-by-step, the reader is taken through the thinking behind each essential concept, and through examples, discussions, and diagrams, shown the full impact on the game's direction. You even learn how to correctly study chess to become a chess master. 400 pages, $19.95.

- BEGINNING CHESS BOOKS -

THE BASICS OF WINNING CHESS *by Jacob Cantrell* - A great first book of chess, in one easy reading, beginner's learn the moves of the pieces, the basic rules and principles of play, the standard openings, and both Algebraic and English chess notation. The basic ideas of the winning concepts and strategies of middle and end game play are shown as well. Includes example games of great champions. 64 pages, $4.95.

BEGINNING CHESS PLAY *by Bill Robertie* - Step-by-step approach uses 113 diagrams to teach novices the basic principles of chess. Covers opening, middle and end game strategies, principles of development, pawn structure, checkmates, openings and defenses, how to write and read chess notation, join a chess club, play in tournaments, use a chess clock, and get rated. Two annotated games illlustrate strategic thinking for easy learning. 144 pages, $9.95

WHIZ KIDS TEACH CHESS *Edited by Eric Schiller*- Ten of today's greatest young stars, ranging from 10-17 years old–some perhaps to be future world champions–present a fascinating look on learning chess. Each tells of their successes, failures, world travels, and love of the game, show off their best moves, and even admit to their most embarrassing blunders. At the heart of this inspirational book targeted toward beginning, under-17 players, is a basic chess primer with large diagrams, clear explanations, and winning ideas. Features Jordy Mont-Reynaud (14), who smashed Bobby Fischer's record by over two years to become the youngest USCF Master, Vinay Bhat (12), Gabe Kahane (16), the Karnazes' twins (10), Irina Krush (15), Asuka Nakamura (11), Hikaru Nakamura (10), and Jennifer Shahade (16). 128 large format pages, $14.95.

- MATES & ENDGAMES -

303 TRICKY CHECKMATES *by Fred Wilson and Bruce Alberston* - Both a fascinating challenge and great training tool, this collection of two, three and bonus four move checkmates is great for advanced beginning, intermediate and expert players. Mates are in order of difficulty, from the simple to very complex positions. Learn the standard patterns and stratagems for cornering the king: corridor and support mates, attraction and deflection sacrifices, pins and annihilation, the quiet move, and the dreaded *zugzwang*. Examples, drawn from actual games, illustrate a wide range of chess tactics from old classics right up to the 1990's. 192 pages, $12.95.

MASTER CHECKMATE STRATEGY *by Bill Robertie* - Learn the basic combinations, plus advanced, surprising and unconventional mates, the most effective pieces needed to win, and how to mate opponents with just a pawn advantage. also, how to work two rooks into an unstoppable attack; how to wield a queen advantage with deadly intent; how to coordinate pieces of differing strengths into indefensible positions of their opponents; when it's best to have a knight, and when a bishop to win. 144 pages, $9.95

BASIC ENDGAME STRATEGY: Kings, Pawns and Minor Pieces *by Bill Robertie* - Learn the mating principles and combinations needed to finish off opponents. From the four basic checkmates using the King with the queen, rook, two bishops, and bishop/knight combinations, to the King/pawn, King/Knight and King/Bishop endgames, you'll learn the essentials of translating small edges into decisive checkmates. Learn the 50-move rule, and the combinations of pieces that can't force a mate against a lone King. 144 pages, $12.95.

BASIC ENDGAME STRATEGY: Rooks and Queens by Bill Robertie - The companion guide to *Basic Endgame Strategy: Kings, Pawns and Minor Pieces*, you'll learn the basic mating principles and combinations of the Queen and Rook with King, how to turn middlegame advantages into victories, by creating passed pawns, using the King as a weapon, clearing the way for rook mates, and other endgame combinations. 144 pages, $12.95.

EXCELLENT CHESS BOOKS - OTHER PUBLISHERS

- OPENINGS -

HOW TO PLAY THE TORRE *by Eric Schiller* - One of Schiller's best-selling books, the 19 chapters on this fabulous and aggressive White opening (1. d4 Nf6; 2. Nf3 e6; 3. Bg5) will make opponents shudder and get you excited about chess all over again. Insightful analysis, completely annotated games get you ready to win! 210 pages, $17.50.

A BLACK DEFENSIVE SYSTEM WITH 1...D6 *by Andrew Soltis* - This Black reply - so rarely played that it doesn't even have a name - throws many opponents off their rote attack and can lead to a decisive positional advantage. Use this surprisingly strong system to give you the edge against unprepared opponents. 166 pages, $16.50.

BLACK TO PLAY CLASSICAL DEFENSES AND WIN *by Eric Schiller* - *Shows you how to develop a complete opening repertoire as black.* Emerge from *any* opening with a playable position, fighting for the center from the very first move. Defend against the Ruy Lopez, Italian Game, King's Gambit, King's Indian, many more. 166 pages, $16.50.

ROMANTIC KING'S GAMBIT IN GAMES & ANALYSIS *by Santasiere & Smith* - The most comprehensive collection of theory and games (137) on this adventurous opening is filled with annotations and "color" on the greatest King's Gambits played and the players. Makes you *want* to play! Very readable; packed with great concepts. 233 pages, $17.50.

WHITE TO PLAY 1.E4 AND WIN *by Eric Schiller - Shows you how to develop a complete opening system as white beginning 1. e4.* Learn the recommended opening lines to all the major systems as white, and how to handle any defense black throws back. Covers the Sicilian, French, Caro-Kann, Scandinavia; many more. 166 pages, $16.50.

MIDDLEGAME/TACTICS/WINNING CONCEPTS -

CHESS TACTICS FOR ADVANCED PLAYERS *by Yuri Averbakh* - A great tactical book. Complex combinations are brilliantly simpified into basic, easy-to-understand concepts you can use to win. Learn the underlying structure of piece harmony and fortify skills through numerous exercises. Very instructive, a must read. 328 pages, $17.50.

STRATEGY FOR ADVANCED PLAYERS *by Eric Schiller* - For intermediate to advanced players, 45 insightful and very informative lessons illustrate the strategic and positional factors you need to know in middle and endgame play. Recommended highly as a tool to learn strategic chess and become a better player. 135 pages, $14.50.

- ENDGAMES -

ESSENTIAL CHESS ENDINGS EXPLAINED VOL. 1 *by Jeremy Silman* - This essential and enjoyable reference tool to mates and stalemates belongs in every chess player's library. Commentary on every move plus quizzes and many diagrams insure complete understanding. All basic positions covered, plus many advanced ones. 221 pages, $16.50.

ESSENTIAL CHESS ENDINGS EXPLAINED VOL. 2 *by Ken Smith* - This book assumes you know the basics of the 1st volume and takes you all the way to Master levels. Work through moves of 275 positions and learn as you go. There are explanations of every White and Black move so you know what's happening from both sides. 298 pages, $17.50.